teach® yourself

ethical living

teach
yourself

stress-free living

ethical living
peter macbride

Launched in 1938, the **teach yourself** series
grew rapidly in response to the world's wartime
needs. Loved and trusted by over 50 million
readers, the series has continued to respond to
society's changing interests and passions and
now, 70 years on, includes over 500 titles,
from Arabic and Beekeeping to Yoga and Zulu.
What would you like to learn?

be where you want to be with **teach yourself**

For UK order enquiries: please contact Bookpoint Ltd, 130 Milton Park, Abingdon, Oxon OX14 4SB. Telephone: +44 (0) 1235 827720. Fax: +44 (0) 1235 400454. Lines are open 09.00–17.00, Monday to Saturday, with a 24-hour message answering service. Details about our titles and how to order are available at www.teachyourself.co.uk

For USA order enquiries: please contact McGraw-Hill Customer Services, PO Box 545, Blacklick, OH 43004-0545, USA. Telephone: 1-800-722-4726. Fax: 1-614-755-5645.

For Canada order enquiries: please contact McGraw-Hill Ryerson Ltd, 300 Water St, Whitby, Ontario L1N 9B6, Canada. Telephone: 905 430 5000. Fax: 905 430 5020.

Long renowned as the authoritative source for self-guided learning – with more than 50 million copies sold worldwide – the **teach yourself** series includes over 500 titles in the fields of languages, crafts, hobbies, business, computing and education.

British Library Cataloguing in Publication Data: a catalogue record for this title is available from the British Library.

Library of Congress Catalog Card Number: on file.

First published in UK 2008 by Hodder Education, part of Hachette Livre UK, 338 Euston Road, London, NW1 3BH.

First published in US 2008 by The McGraw-Hill Companies, Inc.

This edition published 2008.

The **teach yourself** name is a registered trade mark of Hodder Headline.

Typeset by Transet Limited, Coventry, England.
Printed in Great Britain for Hodder Education, an Hachette Livre UK Company, 338 Euston Road, London NW1 3BH, by CPI Cox & Wyman, Reading, Berkshire RG1 8EX.

The publisher has used its best endeavours to ensure that the URLs for external websites referred to in this book are correct and active at the time of going to press. However, the publisher and the author have no responsibility for the websites and can make no guarantee that a site will remain live or that the content will remain relevant, decent or appropriate.

Hachette Livre UK's policy is to use papers that are natural, renewable and recyclable products and made from wood grown in sustainable forests. The logging and manufacturing processes are expected to conform to the environmental regulations of the country of origin.

Impression number   10 9 8 7 6 5 4 3 2 1
Year   2012 2011 2010 2009 2008

contents

introduction		ix
01	**basic ethics**	**1**
	what is 'ethical living'?	2
	making ethical choices	2
	ethical companies	4
	environmental issues	5
	lifetime energy costs and savings	6
	lifetime carbon costs and savings	7
	how do you measure up?	8
	the cost of ethical living	10
	the good neighbour	12
	summary	12
02	**energy**	**13**
	energy sources	14
	energy use in the home	18
	space heating	18
	the low carbon building programme	30
	water heating	31
	lighting	33
	invest in the future	35
	why does efficiency matter that much?	36
	cooking	40
	summary	43
03	**electrical appliances**	**44**
	EU energy labels	45
	washing machines	47

	tumble dryers	47
	dishwashers	48
	fridges and freezers	49
	electronic equipment	51
	computers …	53
	… and printers	54
	how much electricity are you using?	56
	disposal and recycling	57
	summary	58
04	**in the home**	**59**
	water use	60
	invest in the future	61
	cleaning	62
	household waste	70
	paints and varnishes	71
	furniture	75
	floors and floor coverings	78
	summary	79
05	**food and drink**	**80**
	energy and food production	81
	food miles	83
	how can I reduce my food miles?	87
	organic food	99
	food waste	102
	reducing your food waste	103
	food packaging	108
	fairtrade	110
	bottled water	114
	summary	115
06	**shopping**	**117**
	buy less – or even, buy nothing	118
	clothes	119
	gadgets	126
	gifts	129
	plastic shopping bags	131

	ethical retailers and shopping guides	134
	summary	138
07	**money**	**139**
	banking	140
	mortgages	144
	ethical investment	144
	managing your money ethically	146
	summary	146
08	**motoring**	**147**
	do you really need your car?	149
	working with what you've got	152
	total energy costs	155
	alternative fuels	160
	electric (battery) cars	165
	which car?	168
	summary	172
09	**travel and tourism**	**173**
	air travel	174
	tourism	177
	summary	183
taking it further		**184**
index		**186**

Why should you try to lead a more ethical life? Why should you read this book? Crucial questions – and the first is by far the most important. Why should we live ethically? Because, in the long term, it's the only way for us to survive. Ethical living is about sustainability, about not using up irreplaceable resources, about keeping our environment healthy, about dealing fairly with other people. It is based on the recognition that ours is a small planet, and that we need to look after it. Some people have been saying this for years – the Green movement started in the 1960s – though it is only very recently that the problems of global warming, pollution and the over-use of resources entered mainstream awareness, and politicians are still dragging their heels. The danger is that when faced with problems so huge, we tend to throw up our hands and say 'What can we do?' – then either do nothing, or set out to enjoy ourselves while we can. But there are things we can do, and should do.

Which brings us to the second question: Why should you read this book? And the answer is: because it will show you ways in which you can make a difference. There are small changes that we can make to our lifestyle without affecting its quality, but if enough of us make them, the total impact is a real force for good. Some things may seem to be little more than gestures, but gestures count – they help to change the political and social climate. There are also larger changes that we can make. Some of these will require us to make more effort, some to dig deeper into our pockets and some to give up our excesses. You may not be able to make some of these larger changes right now – it may mean a completely different lifestyle for you and your family – but you can at least plan for a more ethical future.

And the future is what it is all about. For the last half-century or so, most of us in the developed countries have enjoyed a standard of living far higher than our ancestors. If we want our children and grandchildren and their descendants to enjoy anything like the same benefits, then we need to start taking better care of the world – and we need to start doing it now!

This book is in four parts. The first chapter sets the scene, giving an overview of the challenges and getting you to assess your own place in the grand scheme of things. The next three chapters look at different aspects of energy, and how we can use less of it, but to better effect. In chapters 05, 06 and 07 we head for the high street to see how we can spend our money ethically – and we'll pop into the bank while we're down there. In the final two chapters we turn to transport and travel: we have become a highly mobile society, at great cost to the environment – we will look at ways to reduce that cost.

Researching this book has made me even more aware of how much our society is living beyond the planet's means. It has also motivated me to make changes to my lifestyle. I hope that reading it motivates you in the same way.

01

basic ethics

In this chapter you will learn:
- about ethical living and ethical choices
- about ethical companies
- about the key environmental issues
- how to assess your environmental footprint
- about the (low) costs of ethical living
- how to start living ethically.

What is 'ethical living'?

Ethical behaviour is that which is good, and we all have an inner voice which tells us what is good. And the basic principles of goodness remain the same, though how they are interpreted into actual behaviour does vary between cultures. An ethical person is one who has concern for the well being of others, and who is aware of the impact of their actions on others. It's in the second part of that – the awareness of impact – where even the best-intentioned of us can fail. On a personal level, we can act with concern for others in a range of ways, from doing good at one end of the scale, to avoiding doing harm at the other.

The focus of this book is on our interactions with the environment and the world at large, rather than on interpersonal behaviour – on how we behave as consumers (and disposers!). For the ethical consumer, this could translate to supporting the local organic farmer, and not buying clothes produced in Burmese sweatshops. On a global level, the ethical person would want to promote international peace, justice and fair trade, and would accept a responsibility to care for the environment. For the ethical consumer this could translate to boycotting companies and countries that abuse human rights, supporting fair trade initiatives and minimizing use of non-renewable resources.

The obvious catch is that it is not always clear – and it is often very difficult to find out – how, with what, and by whom goods have been produced. Being a truly ethical consumer requires a lot of knowledge, regular research and careful thought before every new purchase, and it will have a major impact on your own lifestyle. This book will point you along the road to being a truly ethical consumer, but it will also offer stopping points along the way. If all of us, to a greater or lesser extent, apply an awareness of the ethical and environmental issues to our consumption, then we can help to make the world a better place – for ourselves and for our grandchildren.

Making ethical choices

When you start to apply ethical principles to consumption decisions, you will see that they fall into five broad categories – with a lot of crossing over the boundaries between them:

- **The no-brainer.** Here the ethical issues are clear-cut, and the choice incurs no significant cost and requires no special effort, apart from thinking. A simple example is the use of energy-efficient light bulbs wherever they are suitable – they do cost a little more than the traditional alternatives, but they more than save the difference over their lifespan.

- **The must-do.** With this type of decision, the ethical issues are clear-cut, and should override any considerations of costs, effort, etc. For example, we should not be investing in, buying goods from or going as tourists to states like Burma where a military dictatorship kills and jails its pro-democracy opponents, especially as their leaders have specifically asked outsiders to boycott the country.

- **The worth doing.** This is really a subset of the must-do, and applies where the ethical imperative is not quite so pressing. The ethical issues are again pretty clear, and should be enough to outweigh considerations of slight extra cost, effort or discomfort. Fair trade foods do give third world growers a better deal than they get from mainstream wholesalers, but they often cost a little more than normal and may take a little more effort to find on the shelves. (Minor ethical dilemma: is it better to buy fairtrade bananas from a multinational supermarket or multinational bananas from a local greengrocer?)

- **The calculation.** There are energy/resources decisions which depend upon a number of factors that have to be balanced against one another. For example, the most eco-friendly car may not be the one that uses least petrol per mile, if you look at the total energy and resource usage over its lifetime. The current generation of hybrids take more resources to manufacture, will probably have shorter lifespans and have fewer recyclable components than some of their conventional competitors, and it is questionable whether their better miles per gallon (mpg) makes up for the difference. One of the big problems with this type of decision is that some of the figures may not be knowable, and others will be no more than best estimates.

- **The value-judgement.** There are situations where ethical issues overlap, and it is for each individual to decide which should prevail and to what extent. Where, for example, do you stand in the balance of animal rights against human safety? Would you set an absolute line on this or does it depend on the product? Would you refuse a life-saving drug because it had been tested on animals? How about a routine painkiller, a beauty product, a household cleaner?

Fortunately a lot of decisions fall into the first three categories, and calculations will only normally be needed once a year or so when a larger, long-life purchase is to be made.

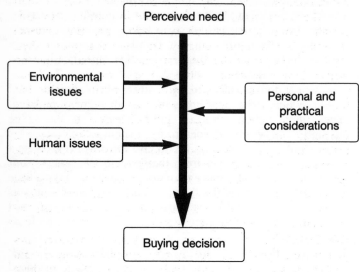

figure 1.1 Factors in the buying decision. Ethical considerations often have to be balanced against personal and practical ones – if you are a professional harpist, it's hard to manage without a Volvo!

Ethical companies

Sometimes what you are buying is less of an issue than who you are buying it from. Read the business pages, and you might be inclined to think that 'ethical company' is an oxymoron – there are certainly some who act as if the pursuit of profit can justify anything.

- **Nobody's perfect.** Some commercial activities are innately unethical. The oil business is the prime example. If a company is in the business of extracting, refining or selling oil, then it is actively contributing to global warming, pollution and the depletion of the earth's scarce resources. The better companies in this field will be working harder to develop alternative energy supplies, to reduce spillages and waste, to encourage careful use, etc. If you have to buy petrol, all you can do is avoid buying from those who are particularly bad or seek out those who make the greatest efforts to be less damaging.

- **It's the company they keep.** Some firms don't seem to mind who they deal with. Those that trade in conflict diamonds bought from West African war lords are the extreme example, but far more common are those that source their toys or clothes from the cheapest possible manufacturer, no matter how low their workers' wages or how bad the working conditions. You will find these firms in all fields, but fortunately, you can normally also find those who *do* have ethical policies about who they will buy from.
- **Corporate greed.** We seem to live in an era where bigger is better and 'greed is good'. Large corporations make enormous profits and these may be fair profits for goods and services supplied. But some have no hesitation in taking the customers for all they can. Some exploit their own workers instead of or as well as their customers, siphoning off the profits into directors' pay and perks.
- **Fair deals.** There are some good companies out there, ones that strive to give a fair deal to their suppliers, workers and customers, and deal in eco-friendly products. Many of these are small, specialist firms, but there are bigger ones – the Co-Op and the John Lewis partnership spring to mind.

Environmental issues

The ethical arguments here are essentially about 'stewardship'. There is nothing unethical, per se, in *using* energy and other resources. The problem lies in *using up* finite resources. We have a duty to future generations – our children and grandchildren, and their children and grandchildren. The earth's resources are finite and too many are being used up at an alarming rate. In the last 100 years, we have used the greater part of the world's known supplies of oil, copper, tin, silver and other key materials, and we are not likely to find large new stores of any of them. We are chopping down the world's great forests, emptying the once-teeming oceans of their fishes and whales, and burning so much coal and oil that we have changed the climate, making it hotter, wetter, wilder, more unpredictable and more damaging.

The rapid rise in CO_2 (carbon dioxide) levels is probably the most urgent problem we face. CO_2 is a part of the natural cycle, absorbed by plants where it is converted into starches, sugars and cellular material, and released through respiration, decay and natural forest and scrubland fires. It is also released – and in damaging quantities – by burning fossil fuels and clearing the great forests. In the 300 years since the start of the Industrial Revolution, concentrations of CO_2 have increased steadily, and have been rising at an exponential rate more recently. CO_2 is being produced at a rate faster than the natural world can absorb it, and levels are now higher than at any time in the last 160,000 years. CO_2 is a 'greenhouse gas', in that it tends to trap the sun's heat. To some extent this is a good thing – without the atmosphere's greenhouse effect we would all freeze to death in the winter (if not every night) – but the current high levels of CO_2 and other greenhouse gases are trapping too much and the earth is overheating.

Using renewable energy has no environmental impact in itself (though it does depend on what you use it for). The sun, wind, tides and rivers could provide all of the world's energy many times over – if these sources could be harnessed.

Food, wood, textile crops and other stuff we can grow are also renewable, but they can have environmental costs which we need to be aware of. Energy goes into their production, processing and distribution. Fertilizers and insecticides can poison the land and the rivers that they drain into. Sustainability is the key word here. Can we continue to replace what we take away in the long term? Can the energy costs be met from renewable sources?

Lifetime energy costs and savings

When you start looking at energy-saving devices, or at energy-generating devices, one of the things you must look at is their lifetime energy costs. How much energy has gone into their manufacture? How much will go into their maintenance during their life, and how much into their disposal at the end of it? These costs must then be balanced against the energy that they will save, or generate, during their working life. It's an exercise well worth doing, because what may seem a good ethical choice may not actually be so.

Domestic wind turbines are a good example of this. In theory, a small turbine can generate more energy than went into its manufacture in under a year, and it will go on generating surplus energy for at least another 30 years. In practice, if you install the turbine on a tower in an open site, exposed to the winds, it will perform to expectations, paying back its energy in the first year. Mount it on the roof of a house in the middle of town, and you will be lucky to generate enough energy to run a single light bulb – the total it produces during its working life will pay back no more than a fraction of its manufacturing energy costs. In the wrong place, a domestic wind turbine is an energy sink, so installing one would be a waste of resources.

Tipping the balance

There may be an argument for buying an 'energy saving/generating' device even though the actual lifetime energy costs/savings balance is negative. Sometimes you need to invest in a new technology to help to get it off the ground. The early models may take more energy to produce because they are not able to benefit from the economies of scale that come with a developed market; they may not deliver all that is hoped, partly because the technology is still in its infancy and partly because their working lives may well be relatively short. The petrol/electric hybrid cars are a good example of this. The models on sale in 2007 are far from being the most energy-efficient cars on the market. More energy and resources are needed for their manufacture and maintenance – for a start, they need two engines (petrol and electric), and many of their components are so complex that they must be replaced, rather than repaired. As for fuel efficiency, there are plenty of cars with better miles per gallon figures – though most of them are smaller. But enough people are buying them to encourage manufacturers to continue developing the next generation of hybrids. (The other very positive aspect of these is that at least some of their buyers are choosing them because they are fashionable. And many of these would otherwise have bought 'Chelsea tractors'.)

Lifetime carbon costs and savings

This refers to how much CO_2 is produced in the manufacture, repair and disposal of a device, compared to how much CO_2 is saved by its use over its lifetime. It's a similar concept to lifetime energy costs, but CO_2 and energy figures are not directly related, especially in manufacturing. The CO_2 saving could come from lower energy use, e.g. insulation which reduces the amount of fuel burnt to heat a house, or it could be a device, such as a wind turbine, which produces little or no CO_2 while it generates electricity.

Embodied energy and embodied carbon

'Embodied energy' refers to the energy that goes into the manufacture of an object; 'embodied carbon' is the CO_2 that was produced during its manufacture. The key problem in assessing these lies in knowing where to draw the line. It's not enough to simply take the total energy used by a factory and divide it by the number of objects produced. You also need to include the energy and CO_2 that went into the manufacture or extraction of the object's components or raw materials, plus that used in its transport, packaging, storage, marketing, and any other processes it goes through.

By themselves, embodied energy and carbon figures are not very meaningful, but where a set of similar objects have been assessed in the same way, the figures do show which is relatively more eco-friendly.

How do you measure up?

Before you go any further, take a few minutes to find out how far you are part of the problem, and how much you need to change if you are to live a sustainable, ethical lifestyle.

Ecological footprint

This is a way to measure your impact on the environment. It calculates how much of the earth's surface is needed to provide the energy, water and other resources that are needed to support your lifestyle, and also how much is required to absorb our carbon emissions and other waste. There are more and less complicated systems for calculating it – and none can ever be entirely accurate – but they do give you a point of comparison. You can compare your lifestyle with that of other people, and perhaps more valuably you can compare your lifestyle now with how it could be if you consumed more ethically.

The average European has a footprint of 6.3 hectares. If everyone on the planet lived at that level, we'd need 3.4 planets.

It could be worse – the average US citizen has a footprint twice as large, so we'd need 6.6 planets for everyone to live the American life. What's your footprint? Best Foot Forward, ecological footprint experts, have a simple calculator on their website at: **http://www.bestfootforward.com/footprintlife.htm**

That takes less than a minute to do. If you have ten minutes, try the Earth Day Footprint quiz at: **http://www.ecofoot.org/**

The quiz itself will only take three or four minutes. But there is a 'Take Action' follow-up where you can see how changes in your lifestyle could reduce your footprint. Even relatively small changes – if you make enough of them – can have quite a large impact.

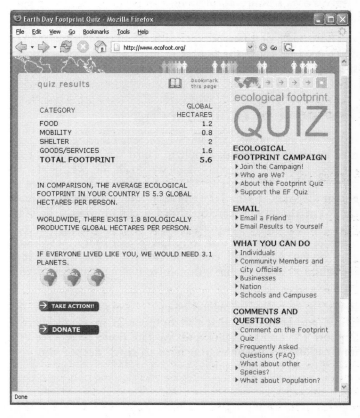

figure 1.2 What's your ecological footprint? Mine could be better – and the Take Action page helped me work out how to reduce it by 1.3 hectares. Take the ecological footprint quiz at **www.ecofoot.org**.

Carbon footprint

This is a subset of the ecological footprint, but with the focus on global warming. It measures the carbon dioxide emissions for which you are responsible, directly through the use of fossil fuels for transport or in the home, and indirectly through your use of services and purchases of goods. The scientific consensus is that to stop global warming we all need to get our CO_2 emissions down to around 2,500 kg per year. Currently, the average in the UK is over 10,000 kg per year, so there's a lot of leeway to make up.

If you want to know your carbon footprint, and what you can do to reduce it, point your browser to:

http:\\www.carbonfootprint.com

You will need some recent fuel bills to hand, as the site will ask you how much of different types of fuel you used in a year. (You don't need to know the figures in litres and tonnes – amount spent or miles travelled will do the job.)

The cost of ethical living

It's an obvious point, but one worth remembering – the poor take less from the world. People in Third World countries have far lower carbon footprints than we do in the West – the US produces over 20 tonnes of CO_2 per capita while, at the other end of the scale, in Chad the emission rate is 0.1 tonnes. And in the West, those who cannot afford a car or foreign holidays have lower footprints than the rich. It's not surprising then that many of the things you can do to lower your footprint will save you money. Most will cost you nothing more than a little thought and effort; some will involve making changes to your lifestyle.

Reducing your environmental impact is a major part of ethical living, and something that can be done at no financial cost. Support for human rights and for fair trade does have cost implications – sometimes you have to reach deeper into your pocket to do the right thing.

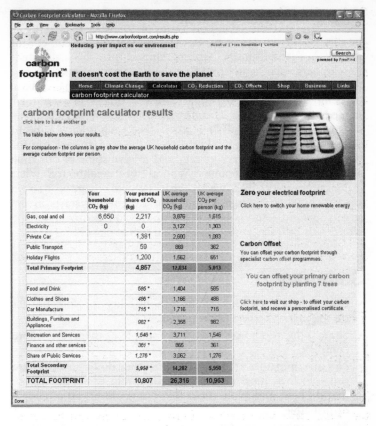

figure 1.3 The carbon footprint website. This site can give you an accurate assessment of your primary carbon footprint – that produced by your direct use of fossil fuels – and offers you two ways to reduce or offset it. It also shows how much of the footprint is derived from secondary sources, but only uses average figures for this. It's worth noting that your share of the carbon dioxide produced by public services amounts to half the target total. Individual efforts are vital, but as a society, we need to do more to reduce our fuel use.

The good neighbour

In this book, the focus is on the practical aspects of ethical living, but the human aspects should not be neglected. Researchers consistently find that the happiest societies are not the wealthiest ones, but those where there is the strongest sense of community – where people care for others beyond their immediate family and friends. Being a good neighbour is important. We should all be ready to lend each other a hand in times of need, to share in taking care of the area, to look out for the very old and the very young, and to give some of our time and energy to the community. Who are our neighbours? What is our community? Well, we all live in a global village now so we need to look far outwards, but your community starts in the streets around your house. What could you do to make the world – or at least, your part of it – a better place?

Summary

- Ethical living is about taking responsibility for your impact on the planet and on other people.
- Some ethical choices are very simple, others are more complex.
- Not all companies are ethical in what they do or how they are run – in fact, most aren't. We should aim to support those that do best, and avoid those that put profit ahead of people or principle.
- The key environmental issue is climate change, and how we can reduce carbon dioxide emissions.
- Assess your own ecological and carbon footprints, and see how far you need to change your way of life.
- Ethical living rarely costs you anything other than effort.
- Being a good neighbour is an important part of ethical living.

02

energy

In this chapter you will learn:
- about the need to cut down fossil fuel use
- how insulation can reduce energy use
- about solar water heating and solar cells
- how to reduce energy use in cooking.

We use energy, of one sort or another, in everything we do. In this chapter, we're looking at energy in the home – how much we use, how we use it, and how we can use less of it.

Energy sources

First of all, where does the energy come from? The best and latest estimates show that in 2004, the UK consumed oil, gas, coal, nuclear electricity and renewable energy totalling the equivalent of over 260 million tonnes of oil.

table 2.1 Energy sources, UK 2004, figure in million tonnes of oil equivalent.

Oil	Gas	Coal	Electricity	Renewable
194	107	40	20	5

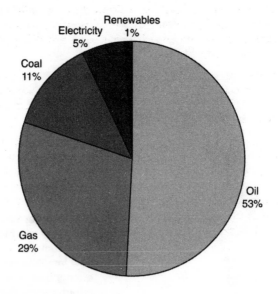

figure 2.1 energy sources, UK 2004.

Oil is by far the most important source of energy for us at the moment, and we must reduce our consumption for two main reasons:

It's running out. We have already taken more out of our own North Sea fields than is left in them, and in the world as a whole we are currently either at or just past peak production. From now onwards, oil will be increasingly scarce.

Burning oil, in vehicle engines or in boilers, produces CO_2 – the main greenhouse gas, and a major factor in climate change.

Gas is mainly used for generating electricity, for space heating and in industry. Like oil, this is a limited resource and its use helps to drive climate change. We have pretty much burnt our way through the gas from the North Sea fields – they will be exhausted within the next 20 years – and we are becoming dependent on imports from Russia and elsewhere.

Coal is almost entirely used for generating electricity. It is a finite resource – they stopped making coal in the Jurassic era – though the world's reserves should last for another couple of hundred years. The crunch point here is that, even with the latest, cleanest technology, coal still produces greenhouse gases when burnt. And if you don't use the latest, cleanest technology, it produces noxious smoke laden with lung-damaging particles, sulphur, and a range of other pollutants.

Electricity in this context refers only to that produced by nuclear power. Currently nearly a fifth of our total electricity is nuclear, but this is declining as old stations reach the end of their safe operational life.

Renewables include wind, solar, hydro, tidal, wood, biomass and other sources of energy that are replenished by nature. Capturing and using the sun's energy, whether as electricity from a solar cell or as wood from a tree, does not add to the greenhouse effect. Instead you become part of the natural cycle. If all our energy came from renewable sources, energy use would not be an issue. But they don't, and so it is.

A nuclear future?

Proponents of nuclear power say that we should be building more new reactors as a way to combat climate change. It's true that they produce very little CO_2 when generating electricity, but there are huge carbon and energy costs in building, maintaining and decommissioning them. And over 50 years since they first started thinking about it, they do not seem to be any closer to solving the problem of how to store radioactive waste safely in the long term – and I do mean long. Some of this stuff will still be dangerous in 25,000 years!

No-brainer

If you have not already done so, switch to a green energy supplier now. It's actually very little trouble (normally). Five minutes online will establish the best green supplier for you – their charges vary according to where you are, though their CO_2 emissions/kWh are the same. Despite expectations, green energy can be cheaper than energy from standard sources. Green electricity is conceivable – it can be generated from hydro-electric schemes, wind farms and other renewables – but is there really such a thing as green gas? Yes, because the gas suppliers offset their carbon emissions, generally by investing in renewable electricity projects.

Teach yourself to save more

If you want to know more about how you can make your home more energy efficient, read *Teach Yourself Saving Energy in the Home*.

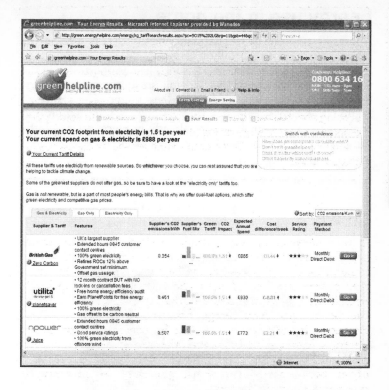

figure 2.2 The green helpline (**www.greenhelpline.com**) is just one of several sites where you can compare gas and electric prices, and then arrange to change your supplier. Other switching sites include uSwitch (**www.uSwitch.com/Energy/Green-Energy.html**) and Energy Watch (**www.energywatch.org.uk**), who also carry good information about just how green these 'green' energy suppliers are.

Energy use in the home

About 30 per cent of the national energy total is used in the home (equivalent to 47 million tonnes of oil) – more than is in industry, though less than in transport. The proportion and the total amount have both been rising steadily over the years, though not, thankfully, as fast as they might. The Office of National Statistics estimates that without the insulation and energy-saving measures that are already in place, we would be using energy at almost twice the current level.

At present, less than 1 per cent of this energy comes from renewable resources. Of the rest, 70 per cent is gas, 21 per cent electric (mostly produced from coal and gas) and 7 per cent oil. Their use is a major part of the UK's CO_2 emissions. We must reduce our use of those finite resources, and we can. But how?

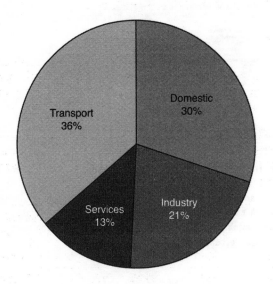

figure 2.3 Energy use in the UK 2004.

Space heating

Space heating accounts for about 60 per cent of the energy used in homes. And a lot of that is wasted. Let's see what we can do.

No-brainer

With some things, the saving of energy – and money – is so obvious, there really is no excuse for not doing them. They take nothing more than a little thought and effort:

- Turning the thermostat down by 1°C could reduce your heating bill by up to 10 per cent, saving around £25 a year, and you probably would not notice the difference.
- Only heat the house when it is needed. Set the timer to come on half an hour before you get up in the morning and before you come home in the evening. Set it to go off half an hour before you go to work, or before you go to bed at night.
- If a room is not normally used, turn its radiator off, and close the door.
- Close the curtains on cold evenings. If the sun's not coming in through the windows, heat is going out.

Must-do

- An un-insulated house wastes a tremendous amount of energy. Insulation costs money, but most forms will repay the investment in as little as two years by dramatically reducing your energy use/heating bills – and the house will be more

Table 2.1 Heat loss and insulation. These figures are all estimates only, and for a typical three-bedroom semi-detached house. The *Heat loss* column shows the estimated percentage of total heat loss through un-insulated walls, loft and windows.

	Heat loss	Cost	Annual saving	Annual CO_2 saving
Cavity wall	33%	£260	£130–£160	1 tonne
Loft (none)	33%	£275	£180–£220	1.5 tonnes
Loft (top up from 5 cm)		£240	£50–£60	0.5 tonnes
Draught proofing	20%	£75+	£20	0.15 tonnes
Secondary glazing (acrylic)	12%	£400	£80–£100	0.7 tonnes

comfortable to live in now that it no longer has cold spots and damp walls. In a typical un-insulated semi-detached house, around one-third of the heat is lost through the walls, one third through the roof, 20 per cent through draughts and poor ventilation, and the rest through the windows.

- The loft should have 25 cm of insulation. If there is nothing there already, this is the most effective step you can take, giving the quickest pay back at low cost.
- Cavity wall insulation is the next best step. This will typically repay its cash investment (and energy cost) in around two years.

What type of insulation?

There are a number of different types of insulation materials that can be used in lofts and cavity walls, and most work in the same way – by trapping air in a loose fibrous or bubbly mass. Fibreglass, mineral wool, polystyrene and polyurethane foam are all equally effective and relatively cheap. Unfortunately they are all derived from petrochemicals, and a lot of embodied energy and carbon goes into their manufacture. There are natural alternatives which will provide the same levels of insulation, but they are not as cheap. This is one of those cases where you do have to reach a little further into your pocket to do the right thing.

Natural insulations include:

- Sheep's wool – a high-performance material, mainly used in lofts. It is sold in batts (slabs) for laying between rafters. It can be used in its full, natural, untreated state, but is normally treated with fire retardants and insect repellent. The leading commercial brand is Thermafleece. To insulate a 20 m^2 loft to a depth of 100 mm would cost around £190, compared to £60 for fibre glass padding.
- Flax and hemp fibres – can be processed into batts or rolls. The product has very low embodied energy, though it has to be chemically treated to protect it from insects and fungi. Its insulating qualities are at least as good as fibre glass, and it also helps to control moisture levels as it can absorb and release humidity without affecting its performance. Examples including Isonat (hemp/cotton) and Isovlas (flax) are readily available. They will both cost around £180 to cover an area 20 m^2 to a depth of 100 mm.
- Newspaper and other cellulose fibres – can be recycled into insulating boards for lofts, or loose fill which can be blown into

cavity walls or spread as loft insulation. Its performance matches that of fibre glass and polystyrene, and the cost is not much more either – around £70 to cover an area 20 m² to a depth of 100 mm. The leading products here are Warmcell and Ecocel.

Suppliers of natural insulations include:

- Eco Merchant at **www.ecomerchant.co.uk**
- Sustainable Building Supplies at **www.sustainablebuilding supplies.co.uk**
- GreenSteps at **www.greensteps.co.uk**
- Calch Ty-Mawr Lime (Welsh Centre for Traditional and Ecological Building) at **www.lime.org.uk**

Worth doing

There are more energy savings to be made. These will take a bit more effort, or longer to recoup their costs, but are still well worth doing:

- Not all rooms need to be the same temperature – the recommended levels are 21°C (70°F) in the living, dining and bathroom, and 18°C (65°F) elsewhere. Room thermostats allow you to control the temperature of each room individually. They will cost around £15 each, plus fitting, but should recoup their cost in a couple of years.
- Turn the thermostat down 2 or 3°C and you can cut a further 10 per cent from your heating bills. And if you or anyone else in the family does feel the cold, you will have saved enough to buy some woolly jumpers. Realistically, should you expect to be able to sit around in your shirtsleeves in the winter? Is it a hardship to wear warmer clothes?
- Draught proofing windows and doors is inexpensive. The savings are not great, but it will make rooms more comfortable. Just don't overdo it! You need some air circulation, especially if there is a gas fire in the room.

Calculate the cost

On the heating and insulation front there are two areas where you may need to think carefully before you make changes: the boiler and the windows. If you are building a new house, or replacing a worn-out boiler or a rotted window frame, there is no problem – you go for the most energy-efficient solution. But if you are thinking about replacing something which still has a useful life, this has environmental implications. You have to balance the carbon and energy costs of manufacturing the new equipment, and of disposing of the old ones, against the savings once they are installed. (And there are financial implications. Both a new boiler and double glazing involve substantial investments, which will pay for themselves in the long term, but not in the next few years. If you intend moving in the near future, you need to be aware that they won't normally add enough to the sale price of the house to cover their costs.)

Gas boilers

Since 2005, you have only been allowed to install a boiler with an efficiency rating of A or B on the SEDBUK scale (Seasonal Efficiency of Domestic Boilers in the UK sets the British standards), and that basically means a condensing boiler. These condense the exhaust gases, capturing much of the heat that would otherwise go up the flue, and pass it back into the water heating system. In theory, a condensing boiler can achieve 90 per cent efficiency, but that is only under optimal conditions, with the equipment operating at its peak. These boilers are more complex than the traditional alternative, have more to go wrong and need more frequent servicing to keep at their best, so in practice, you should assume an efficiency closer to 80 per cent. That is about 10 to 15 per cent better than a properly-maintained traditional boiler.

Condensing boilers are relatively new technology, and so far we have only estimates of their lifespan, but their extra complexity makes it likely that they won't last the 25 years that you would expect from a traditional one. This hits the cost-balance. A new boiler will cost between £1,500 and £2,250 to install. If you have already done the 'no-brainer', 'must-do' and 'worth doing' energy-saving steps then your current heating bills will have already been reduced – perhaps down to £500 or £600 p.a. on a family home. On current energy prices, a 15 per cent increase in efficiency would deliver savings of under £100 and would take 15 to 25 years to recoup the investment. Energy prices are highly likely to continue to rise, so the effective payback time could be within the life of the boiler. The energy payback time – that saved by its use compared to the energy used in its manufacture – should be considerably shorter.

Alternative 1: Wood stoves and boilers

Wood is a carbon-neutral fuel, in that it absorbs as much CO_2 while it's growing as it releases when it's burnt. And if the wood comes from a managed source, then the cycle continues.

Slow burners produce a cosy, steady heat, but are not good for the environment, as the slow, low temperature produces smoke, containing particulates and toxic gases. You need a modern, fast-burning stove. These reach very high temperatures to give almost 100 per cent combustion, burning off pollutants, reducing particles to a minimum – and producing very little ash. The stoves are designed to absorb the heat into their bodies, and then release it slowly. In typical use, the stove would be laid and lit at the start of the day; the burn would be complete within an hour or so, then the stove would radiate out heat for the rest of the day.

If you want to run central heating from wood, you can use a stove with a back boiler, but you are probably better off with a boiler, and preferably one that runs on wood chips or pellets (processed waste from sawmills). These can be set to run automatically, with the fuel stored in a hopper and fed in on demand.

A good, reliable source of supply is essential if you are contemplating wood as a fuel. And you need storage space. Logs must be stored for a minimum of two years, and preferably more, before they are used, as wet wood produces smoke and pollutants, however it is burned. If you do not have the space for two years' worth of wood, then you need someone who can supply you with seasoned wood – though you will still need room enough for the minimum delivery. With chips or pellets, the question is whether there is a supplier in your area – having it delivered from the other side of the country is not an eco-friendly option!

Wood is a cheaper fuel than either gas or electricity – about 25 per cent cheaper when used as a room heater, and up to 50 per cent in a central heating system.

figure 2.4 There are lots of wood stove suppliers, and even the smaller firms also seem to sell online. Stoves Are Us (**www.stovesareus.co.uk**) – whose website is shown here – and Stove Centre (**www.stovecentre.co.uk**) both carry wide selections of types and sizes; Firebelly Stoves (**www.firebellystoves.com**) sell very smart stoves and wood pellet boilers.

Alternative 2: Heat pumps

Heat pumps are refrigerators in reverse – at least, they are the reverse in their effect, but the technology is identical. A heat pump draws low grade heat from one source and transfers it, as higher grade heat, to another. In a fridge, it takes heat from inside and radiates it out the back; in a domestic heat pump, it takes heat from outside and brings it into the house. It's all based on the thermal qualities of gas – if you compress gas, it gets hotter and will radiate out the heat; if you expand it, it gets cooler and will absorb any heat from its surroundings. It is a highly efficient system, producing 3 to 4 kilowatts of heat for every 1 kW used to power the pump.

Domestic heat pump systems are usually geothermal – they draw their heat from the ground. In the UK, the ground rarely freezes more than a spade's depth down, and once you get below about 1 metre, its temperature is pretty constant, and can typically range from 7°C to 13°C. This is a viable heat source, especially as the ground has such thermal mass that you can draw from it steadily throughout the colder months without significantly lowering its temperature. The heat-collector is normally a continuous run of flexible piping, laid horizontally about 1 metre below the surface. If you do not have sufficient area available, the pipework can be installed vertically – which needs more specialized equipment. The heat pump itself is the size of a large boiler. It can be fitted to an exterior wall, or tucked into the garage.

Heat pumps are best used with underfloor heating. They can be used with radiators, but because they don't get the water as hot as a boiler will, you need more or bigger radiators to heat the same space.

Once installed, the system should need minimal maintenance – when did you last have to do anything to your fridge, apart from clearing out uneaten food? The pipework should be good for at least 50 years, and heat pumps have a life expectancy of 25+ years.

The best time to fit a ground heat pump system is when a house is being built, so that you have clear access to the land and the necessary diggers and earth-moving equipment is on site. As part of a new build, a system suitable for a three-bedroom detached house would cost around £5,500 – and you would not need a boiler as this will deliver all the space heating and hot water that you need. Retro-fitted into an existing house, the costs go up, and you would probably be looking at closer to £8,000. (These prices take into account the grants that you can get for low carbon installations.)

The savings are good. You will be using up to 75 per cent less energy to heat your home, and with electricity from a green supplier, that will mean zero CO_2 emissions. You should save

£400 to £600 a year in energy bills, so that even at current prices, even a retro-fit system would pay for itself in 20 years or less. With a new build, the savings are far higher because you can also deduct the cost of the boiler that would otherwise have been needed. The system would pay for itself totally in less than ten years, and then continue to deliver big savings for another 40 years or more.

To get a better idea of prices and designs, visit one or more of these sites: Ice Energy (**www.iceenergy.co.uk**), Earth Energy (**www.earthenergy.co.uk**) or Eco heat pumps (**www.ecoheat pumps.co.uk**).

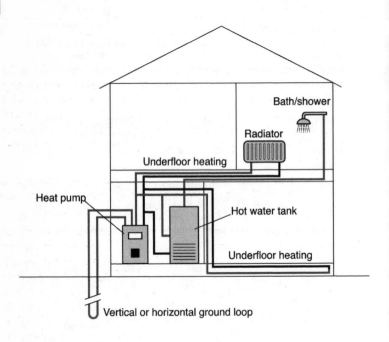

figure 2.5 The ground beneath our houses is a reliable – and renewable – source of heat.

Double-glazing

Single-glazed windows radiate heat to the great outdoors. Double-glazed windows also radiate heat, though at only half the rate. The U values tell the story – these describe the amount of heat that passes through a material. Let's consider these figures:

Material	U value
Single pane	5.6
Double-glazed*	2.8
Solid wall	1.6
Filled cavity wall	0.35

*The 2.8 figure is for a standard double-glazed pane with a 12 mm air gap. This can be lowered to 2.0 by increasing the air gap to 20 mm, or by using Pilkington K glass, which has a special heat reflecting coating, for the inner pane. Triple glazing will lower the U value a little more, but nothing will bring a window down to the level of a cavity wall. However, there is a second factor to bear in mind.

Windows also let in light and heat. The heat gain through a south-facing double-glazed window over the winter months can be equal to the heat loss, so their effective U value is zero.

But back to the question of 'is it worth doing?' In terms of energy saving, you certainly need some form of secondary glazing, but proper double glazing is expensive. For a family home, the saving will only be around £100 a year, but the cost is likely to be between £3,000 and £4,000. Even with rising energy prices, you probably will not recoup the investment within the lifetime of the windows (of which more shortly). Secondary internal glazing, using acrylic sheet, or glass, in plastic or metal frames, should cost under £500 as a DIY job, or around £1,000 professionally done. The main advantages of double glazing over secondary glazing are convenience and appearance – cleaning can be more difficult, it can be more awkward to open windows and you have a double set of frames.

If you do decide to invest in double-glazed windows, do not be seduced by the claims of uPVC frames. uPVC is not an environmentally friendly material. The manufacture of uPVC is energy intensive and has toxic by-products – six of the 15 most hazardous chemicals listed by European governments for priority elimination are released during its production and disposal. Though they are advertised as maintenance-free, in practice the frames only have a lifespan of 20 to 25 years before they begin to go brittle. And once they do start to go, they cannot be repaired, but must be replaced completely.

Frames made of treated softwood have expected lifetimes of 25 to 30 years, even with only basic maintenance. Properly looked after, their lives can be extended far longer, and any patches of rot or wear can be repaired. Wood frames do not cost more than uPVC, and may even be cheaper. Shop around – but do make sure that the wood comes from a managed source.

Patio heaters

Gas and electric patio heaters are very wasteful of energy. Much of that heat is carried away instantly by movements of the air; the rest is radiated out again as it is absorbed. Home use is increasing, and with the smoking ban in pubs and restaurants, which came into force in 2007, we now face an explosion in their use. One patio heater running all evening (and some lunchtimes), through much of the year can produce almost 4 tonnes of CO_2 a year: that's around two-thirds of an average household's total emissions. If you are cold when sitting outside, put a jumper on. If some form of heating is necessary, buy a wood-burning chimenea.

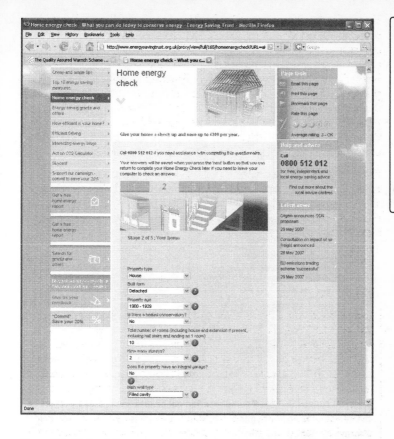

figure 2.6 Find out the energy requirements of your home – and what you can do to reduce them at the Energy Saving Trust. Go to **www.energysavingtrust.org.uk** and follow the links to Home energy check. It takes five minutes or so to work through the questionnaire.

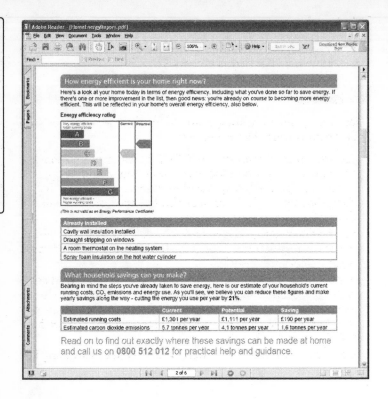

Adobe Reader - [HomeEnergyReport.pdf]

File Edit View Document Tools Window Help

Find:

How energy efficient is your home right now?

Here's a look at your home today in terms of energy efficiency, including what you've done so far to save energy. If there's one or more improvement in the list, then good news: you're already on course to becoming more energy efficient. This will be reflected in your home's overall energy efficiency, also below.

Energy efficiency rating

Very energy efficient - lower running costs | Current | Potential

A
B
C
D
E
F
G

Not energy efficient - higher running costs

(This is not valid as an Energy Performance Certificate)

Already installed

| Cavity wall insulation installed |
| Draught stripping on windows |
| A room thermostat on the heating system |
| Spray foam insulation on the hot water cylinder |

What household savings can you make?

Bearing in mind the steps you've already taken to save energy, here is our estimate of your household's current running costs, CO_2 emissions and energy use. As you'll see, we believe you can reduce these figures and make yearly savings along the way - cutting the energy you use per year by **21%**.

	Current	Potential	Saving
Estimated running costs	£1,301 per year	£1,111 per year	£190 per year
Estimated carbon dioxide emissions	5.7 tonnes per year	4.1 tonnes per year	1.6 tonnes per year

Read on to find out exactly where these savings can be made at home and call us on **0800 512 012** for practical help and guidance.

2 of 6

figure 2.7 After you have completed the questions, you will get a report on the energy efficiency of your home, with suggestions as to how you could improve it, and by how much.

The low carbon building programme

This is a government initiative which provides grants for PV systems, wind turbines, solar water heating, and ground source heat pumps for microgeneration technologies. It is grossly under-funded, and grants are distributed on a first-come-first-get basis, so get your application in early. Maybe by the time you read this, the government will have decided it is time to really put some money into developing renewable energy systems, and things will have improved. We can only hope – or vote for parties that do have a proper green agenda. For details, go to **www.lowcarbonbuildings.org.uk**.

Water heating

On average 23 per cent of domestic energy is used for heating water. How much of that is necessary?

No-brainer

There's no point in heating more water than we need, or to a higher temperature than is needed:

- Set your tank thermostat to 60°C, which is more than hot enough for any domestic purposes. You could drop it a couple of degrees below this, but it must not be run below 55°C, because bacteria, such as those that cause Legionnaires disease, can survive up to there.
- Set the timer so that the water heats up for when you need it, but is off for the rest of the day. With a well-insulated tank, there is very little heat loss.
- A shower typically uses less than half as much hot (and cold) water as a bath, though power showers use about the same amount. (If your shower is in the bathtub, you can easily test this. Put the plug in next time you have a shower and see how full the bath gets.)
- Don't wash yourself – or anything else – under a running hot tap.

Must-do

Few houses nowadays have un-insulated hot water tanks – for some years now, most have been prefitted with a solid foam jacket. If you have a loose jacket, check its depth – it should be at least 10 cm. Replacing a thin or badly fitting jacket will cost around £15 and pay for itself in two years.

Worth doing

Solar water heating is a viable option that we should all be considering. The technology is now well developed, and the benefits proven. It can deliver up to 90 per cent of a house's hot water in the summer, and capture some heat even in the winter. Overall, you can expect to reduce your water heating bills by around 70 per cent in the UK. A two-panel system, suitable for a family of four, will cost a little over £3,000 to install and should save about £80 p.a. A solar system will recover its embodied energy in three to five years, and its embodied carbon in seven to ten years. At current prices, it would take over 30 years to recoup the investment, but as energy prices are likely to rise, the actual payback time will probably be much less.

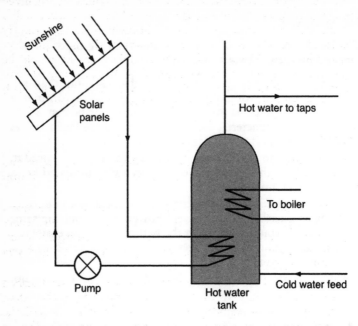

figure 2.8 A basic solar system. A fluid is pumped through the collector panels, then through a coil in the hot water tank. The tank also has a second coil, heated by a standard boiler, to be used as necessary.

Install with care

It is not difficult to install your own solar water heating system. The components are readily available – you can even make your own, (reasonably efficient) collector plates – and installation is within the scope of any competent handyman, as long as you are happy to work on the roof. An unfortunate side effect of this is that the business tends to attract more than its fair share of cowboys. If you are going to have a professional installation, don't just get at least three quotes. Make sure that you also go and look at, and talk to the owners of, systems that the firms have installed previously.

Lighting

The electricity used in lights and appliances adds up to around 12 per cent of the total energy used in a home. Few of these use much energy individually, so the potential savings on any given usage is quite small, but this is a case of 'many a mickel makes a muckel'. For example, if every household in the country replaced five standard 100 watt bulbs with the equivalent energy-efficient 20 watt bulbs, the combined saving would be over 5,000 Megawatts and we could shut Drax, the largest coal-fired power station in the UK. This would reduce our CO_2 emissions by over 20 million tonnes! Every little helps!

No-brainer

- Walk round the house. Take a note of every light and appliance, and ask yourself, 'Does this need to be on?' If not, turn it off.
- Get into the habit of turning lights off as you leave the room. A single 100 watt light bulb burning for six hours every evening, will use 0.6kWh (kilowatt hours) of electricity a day, costing about 4p. That's not much, but turn it off and you save 200 kWh of electricity (£14) a year!
- Turn off the TV, radio and computer when you have finished using them – and turn them off completely, rather than leaving them on standby. It's estimated that in the UK the total energy consumed by appliances on standby is responsible for one million tonnes of CO_2 emissions. Do you know, the average video player uses 85 per cent of its energy while it's on standby – doing nothing. Turn them off!

Must-do

In a standard tungsten light bulb, the majority of the energy is transformed into heat, and less than 20 per cent into visible light. Fluorescent tubes are far more efficient, converting virtually all of the energy into light – but, until recently, it wasn't the sort of light that people wanted in the living areas of their homes. The cold, faintly blue light was acceptable in offices and shops, and even in utility rooms, kitchens and bathrooms, but not elsewhere. Their long thin shapes also limited the places in which they could be used. The first CFL (compact fluorescent light) bulbs were not that much better – the quality of the light was still harsh, and the U-shaped tubular bulb was too long to fit comfortably into many light fittings.

Things have changed. The new generation of CFL bulbs produce a quality of light that is at least as warm and natural as that from a tungsten bulb, and they are available as twisted tubes, or enclosed bulbs the same shape as tungsten ones. The only two drawbacks to the latest CFL bulbs is that they do not instantly give full brightness when you switch them on (they take about a second to get there), and that most cannot be used with dimmer switches (though you can now buy ones which can be dimmed).

The numbers speak for themselves:

- Tungsten bulbs cost around 30p and have a life of about 1,000 hours – a year of average use. A 100 watt bulb will use 100 kilowatts of electricity during its life, at a cost of just over £7.
- CFL bulbs cost around £3.50 and have a life of about 8,000 hours. An 18 watt bulb will give the same light output as a 100 watt tungsten bulb. In 1,000 hours it will use 18 kilowatts of electricity, at a cost of just over £1.20.

Long before you have reached the end of the first year, the energy saving will have covered the extra cost of the CFL bulb. Over the lifetime of the CFL bulb, it will use £10 of electricity, while its eight tungsten equivalents will use £56.

A couple of minor points about energy-saving bulbs:

- Because they use so much less energy, people may be less diligent about turning them off when not needed. Keep reminding yourself, your family, friends and colleagues – if it's not needed, turn it off!
- Fluorescent bulbs contain a small but significant amount of mercury. They should not be thrown away with the general rubbish, but should go to a suitable recycling centre. However, even if this mercury is released into the atmosphere, it would be far less than would be produced by a coal-fired power station in generating enough energy to light tungsten bulbs over the life of that dead CFL.

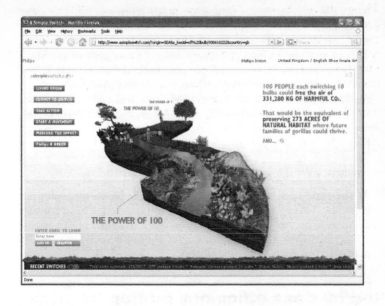

figure 2.9 If you want to get a better idea of the difference you can make by switching to energy-saving bulbs, or you want some mind-boggling statistics to quote at people, head to **www.asimpleswitch.com**. This is a site run by Philips, with the aim of encouraging the use of energy-saving bulbs (made by Philips, naturally). It's worth a visit just to see the great graphics!

Invest in the future

Electricity from the sun

Solar cells, properly called photovoltaic (PV) cells generate electricity from sunlight – and though they work best in full sunlight, they can still generate in cloudy weather, as long as there is some daylight. They are unobtrusive and silent in operation. Once installed, they should require no maintenance for the rest of their 30+ years' life, and over that time a typical domestic PV system could save over 30 tonnes of CO_2 emissions.

Most PV cells currently in use are made from silicon. The most efficient, and most expensive, are the monocrystalline silicon cells, which contain a wafer of silicon cut from a single crystal. These can convert into electricity up to 15 per cent of the sun's energy that falls on them (15 per cent may not sound much, but coal or gas power stations only convert around 30 per cent of the fuel's energy into electricity). Multicrystal cells are cheaper to produce, but a little less efficient. All crystalline silicon panels are rigid and relatively heavy. At the other end of the scale, thin film PV uses a layer of silicon deposited on a flexible sheet. These are much cheaper to produce, but considerably less efficient, averaging around 6 per cent conversion.

At the time of writing, new thin film cells, based on cadmium telluride (CdTe) and copper indium diselenide (CIS) are under development but not yet on the open market. Both show efficiencies over 15 per cent, and yet should be even cheaper to manufacture than thin film silicon.

Why does efficiency matter that much?

There are two key reasons why efficiency matters:

- The first relates to how much electricity you can generate off your roof. In the UK, a 15 per cent efficiency system needs something over 1.5 m^2 to produce 1 kW a day under optimum conditions; a 6 per cent efficiency system would need nearly 5 m^2 for the same output.

- The second relates to payback times. The PV industry talks in general terms, of a 20-year (financial) payback on solar cells – the energy payback time is less than half of that – but you can only get sensible figures by looking at individual installations. The vertical angle and orientation to the sun, and the shade cast by neighbouring buildings and trees all affect the amount of energy produced by a PV system. The type of installation and whether the system is being added to an existing house or built into the structure of a new one, all affect the cost. When you are planning a system, don't just get quotes from different suppliers, get them for different materials, and make sure that you also get realistic, measured, calculated projections of electricity production.

Practical matters

The thing about solar cells is that they generate electricity most when you need them least – unless you work from home and use electrical equipment, or watch a lot of daytime TV. The other notable thing about them is that they produce DC (direct current) electricity – what you get from batteries, rather than AC (alternating current) that you get from the mains. The net result is that what you get out of PV cells is not exactly what you need.

If you leave the output as DC, it restricts their use to charging batteries or to powering equipment that runs off DC. There are more of these than you might guess at first – basically anything which normally works off batteries, or which has an AC–DC transformer, which includes computers and most of their peripherals, radio and hifi equipment, mobile phones, some types of lights, and much else.

If you attach an inverter to the cells, this will convert the DC to AC power, and you can feed the output directly into the mains. This is the simple solution, but inverters do add to the cost of the system and reduce the output slightly – there is some loss of power during conversion.

There are several solutions to the time-based production/need dilemma. The most common is to connect your installation to the national grid. When you are generating more than you are using, the excess flows into the grid – in effect, winding your metre backwards – and when you are not generating enough for your needs, you draw it from the grid as usual. (In Germany, they pay a premium for PV energy, currently four times the normal going rate, and this has encouraged the widespread take up of solar systems. In the UK, the rates are not as generous at present, but we can always hope for a more positive approach in the not too distant future.)

The solution which makes the most efficient use of your solar electricity can only really be implemented if you are designing and equipping the house from scratch, with a bank of batteries in the cellar, a DC mains circuit and appliances that run on DC power.

Mounting options

On an existing house, the best solution is normally a set of panels, mounted above the roof. Ideally, it should face due south, but it could be as far round as south east or south west without reducing the output by more than a few per cent. There is also an ideal pitch – this depends upon the latitude of the site, but will be around 30° in the UK. If the roof is flat, the panels can be mounted on an angled bracket. And if there is no suitable south-facing roof, it is possible to mount panels at an angle on a wall.

PV cells can also be fitted in place of normal roof tiles. The units are typically the width of four tiles, and the depth of one or two, and can be fitted to the standard battens.

There are also façade materials, with built-in thin-film PV cells, which can be used for external wall cladding. Their striking appearance makes these more suitable for office blocks than for domestic buildings.

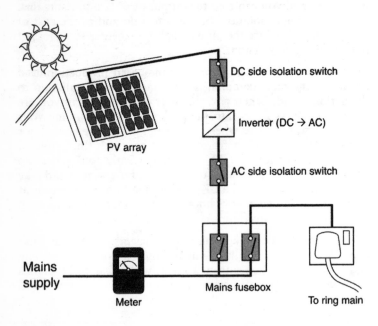

figure 2.10 The elements of a typical roof-mounted PV system, linked to the mains supply.

Outputs and costs

The output from a PV system is rated in Wp (peak Wattage) – its maximum. As the maximum is only reached in ideal conditions, and only for part of each day even then, the more useful measure is kWh p.a. –kilowatt hours per year. A typical two-panel 100 Wp installation on a well-lit site will generate around 1,500 kWh per year. That's about 5 kWh per day, or an average of 1 kW an hour during the evenings. You could generate enough to run your (low-energy) lights and a TV or PC. At current prices, the value is a little over £100 per year. As such systems cost over £12,000, the financial return does not look good – less than 1 per cent – but that's not the whole story. There are government grants available for householders, and these can cover up to 50 per cent of the cost. The grants are, at present, in short supply – you have to work at it, and be lucky, to get one. Secondly, electricity prices will almost certainly rise in the future. With a grant and higher prices, a PV installation is probably a good long-term investment even in purely financial terms. In energy terms, it is certainly a good investment as long as you have a suitable site.

Solar electricity systems will get cheaper and more efficient. Once the thin-film PV technology reaches the mass production stage, we should see a distinct drop in the cost of systems, and an improvement in their efficiency.

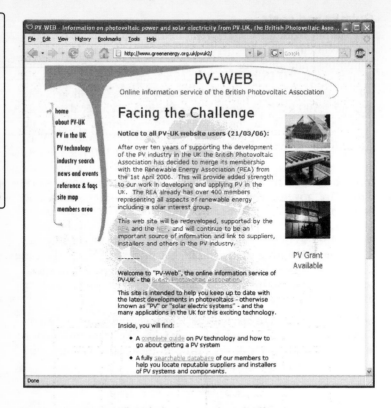

figure 2.11 PV Web is the online information service of the British Photovoltaic Association. It's got lots of information about the technology, the systems, government grants and suppliers. Visit them at **www.greenenergy.org.uk/pvuk2**.

Cooking

On average, cooking takes around 3 per cent of the energy used in our homes. That doesn't leave a lot of room for major savings, but the kitchen should not be ignored.

When you are measuring the efficiency of a cooking method, what you are looking at is the transfer of heat to food – which may sound a bit obvious, but there is a point to this.

Cookers

For (hot) ovens, the most efficient system is fan-assisted electric, which will cook about 20 per cent faster than a normal electric or gas oven. Microwave ovens are far more efficient than any hot oven, simply because virtually all of their energy goes into heating the food, and hardly any into the food's container or the surrounding air or the oven's body. They can use as little as 10 per cent of the amount of energy as a conventional electric oven to cook the same quantity of food.

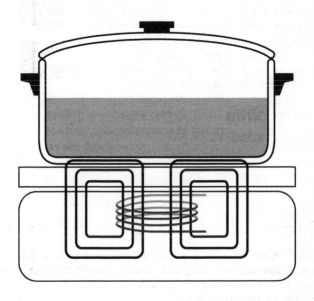

figure 2.12 Cooking by induction. This works by heating the pan directly, not by heating the hob. A high-power electromagnet in the hob induces a magnetic field in the pan, generating an electric current within the metal. The resistance to the current heats the pan, just as an electric coil gets hot because of its resistance. It's highly controllable – the current can go from 2 or 3 kilowatts to nothing instantly – and the hob itself does not get hot, except from having a hot pan sitting on it.

The pan must be iron or steel for this to work, though you can get iron base plates to put beneath copper or aluminium pans (and that must reduce the efficiency).

On the hob, gas is more efficient than most types of electric cookers, because it is more controllable, but an electric induction hob is twice as efficient as gas. (According to the US Department of Energy, induction hobs have an efficiency of 84 per cent, while gas hobs are slightly under 40 per cent – and electric coil hobs are about half of that.)

Worth doing

With any types of cookers, good practice can reduce energy use:

- Don't open the oven door any more than necessary. Every time you open it, you lower the inside temperature and increase the cooking time. If there is a glass door, turn on the light and check the food by looking.
- Turn off electric ovens several minutes before the end of the cooking time. It will stay hot enough to finish cooking, as long as the door stays closed.
- On the hob, use pans the same size as the ring, as far as possible. With a small pan on a large ring, much heat is lost up the sides.
- Put lids on pans unless there is a reason not to. Water will come to the boil faster, and will need less heat to keep boiling with the lid on.

Kettles

The key here is not to boil any more water than you need at the time. There are two sides to this:

You need a kettle that can boil a small amount – and that means either an old-fashioned metal one that goes on the hob, or an electric one with the element below the base plate. If you have to cover an exposed element, that takes a minimum of a couple of cups.

You have to get into the habit of only putting in what you need. Most of the electric 'jug' kettles have measuring scales on a clear window or on the inside.

If you live in a hard water area, you need to keep limescale under control. Scale on the element or base plate will reduce efficiency. To remove it, put enough vinegar into the kettle to cover the limescale and leave overnight, then rinse out in the morning.

Buying guide

When you next buy a new kettle, bear these things in mind:

- A clear plastic window with a scale gives you better control over how much water you heat.
- If it will sometimes be used to boil small amounts of water – a cup of tea for one – get a model with a concealed element.
- Some have LED lights built in that glow constantly, but change colours to indicate when they are on/off/boiled. Very pretty, but not a good addition. They are a waste of energy, both in manufacturing and in use, and can fail – the inside of a kettle is a harsh environment for electronics.
- Some have a 'keep warm' facility. This is a waste of energy. Boil what you need, when you need it.
- An insulated body will keep water hot longer, reducing the need for reboiling. There are several insulated kettles on the market, and though they may be a little more expensive, they should repay this in lower running costs.

Summary

- The bulk of our energy currently comes from fossil fuels, and this must change – oil and gas are running out fast, and the greenhouse gases produced by burning fossil fuels are the main cause of global warming.
- We must decrease our energy use overall, and derive more of our energy from renewable sources.
- The main use of energy in the home is for heating space. Good insulation is essential, and repays its costs rapidly.
- Solar water heating is a long-term investment well worth thinking seriously about.
- Energy-efficient light bulbs save money as well as electricity!
- You can generate your own electricity with solar cells systems. The technology is improving and prices are falling steadily.
- Cookers and kettles may not use a lot of energy, but there are useful savings to be made with both.

03

electrical appliances

In this chapter you will learn:
- about manufacturing energy and usage energy
- about EU energy labels
- how to find out the energy costs of appliances
- how to run your appliances more efficiently
- how to measure your electricity use.

There are two aspects to and two questions about energy use with any electrical appliance. The first, and most obvious, is the energy needed to run it, and how you can minimize that. The second is the energy that went into its manufacture, and how you can get maximum value out of that. The first aspect is the easiest to tackle – it's simple to find out how much energy an appliance uses when it is running, and simple to control how much it runs. We'll look at this more closely as we work through different types of appliances.

The second aspect is much more difficult – there are no reliable, comparable published figures that will tell you how much energy goes into making appliances. However, there are some handy rules of thumb for maximizing the use of this energy, and they apply to all types of equipment:

- Use it until it dies. The only exception to this is where you have a very inefficient old appliance and can replace it with one which will do the same job using, say, half the energy.
- Simpler is better. Every extra function, gadget or option built into an appliance took energy to develop and manufacture and is another thing to go wrong, potentially reducing its lifespan (see point 1).
- Beware cheap and cheerful. If it's cheaper because it's simpler (see point 2), that's good; if it's cheaper because it's less well-made, that's bad. If you pay 20 per cent more but get an appliance which will last 50 per cent longer – well, you do the maths. Before you go out to buy new equipment, check the recent *Which?* reports, especially their readers' surveys. These will give you a good idea about which manufacturers and which models are most reliable.

EU Energy Labels

By law, the European Community Energy Label must be displayed on all new household products of the following types displayed for sale, hire or hire-purchase:

- refrigerators, freezers and fridge-freezers
- washing machines
- electric tumble dryers
- combined washer-dryers
- dishwashers

- lamps
- electric ovens
- air conditioners

The labels all have the key energy rating at the top, but then vary according to the type of appliance. If it meets other environmental criteria, the appliance may have been awarded the Ecolabel Flower – seen here to the right of the energy rating.

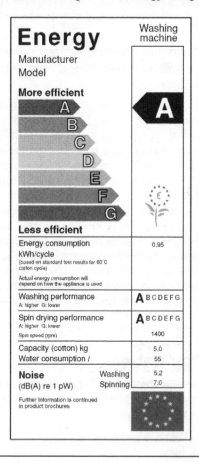

Washing machines

Heating the water is what takes the energy in a washing machine – agitating and spinning the drum take relatively little. So, if you want to save energy, that is where to start. Your machine will probably have a 95°C setting, but this should never be needed – the clothes will come out as clean from a 60°C wash, and the machine will use half the electricity. Most of the time, a 30°C wash will do the job perfectly well, though you may need to switch to a washing powder that is designed for lower temperatures.

If you can, fill with hot water from your heating system, which will normally be more efficient than the washing machine's heater.

Select the shortest, coolest cycle that will do the job.

If there is a half-load setting, use it thoughtfully. It takes more than half as much water and electricity to run a half wash, so if possible, wait until you have a full load.

Buying guide

When choosing a new washing machine, check the energy labels. You want one that has an A rating for energy efficiency and which uses the least amount of water, proportionate to the load size. The difference between the most and the least efficient is quite marked – from 1.2 kWh to 2 kWh for the same washing cycle. A 30° option is essential. A half-load setting will be useful if there are times when you need to wash small quantities.

Tumble dryers

The sun and wind do a better job for drying clothes – and that's all totally renewable energy! But if you have no garden, this is not an option. Gas-heated tumble driers are more energy efficient, though more expensive.

Dishwashers

Let's start with some good news: if you have a lot of washing up to do, it is more energy efficient to do it in the dishwasher than by hand. Why? Because the dishwasher will use considerably less hot water to get the same results. (According to calculations by Electrolux, dishwashers use only 20 per cent of the water of hand washing, but you do need to add in the energy costs of building, running and disposing of the machine).

Two tips for optimum energy-efficiency:

- Wait until you have a full load – if there is going to be a long delay before the other half of the load will appear, run a short rinse cycle so that food doesn't dry hard onto the plates.
- It takes more energy to dry dishes than to wash them, so let them dry naturally. If your machine does not have no-dry option, stop the cycle after the last draining and open the door to let the dishes air dry.

Buying guide

Dishwashers fall into two main categories – undercounter and slimline. Undercounter models typically have space for 12 settings, and have fairly similar performance in terms of energy use – the most efficient ones use 1 kWh of electricity and 14 litres of water per cycle; the least efficient uses 1.24 kWh and 19 litres – that's 35 per cent more water, but only 20 per cent more electricity. Slimline models typically take eight settings, but show more variation in their efficiency. The best use 0.74 kWh of electricity per cycle while the worst uses 1.1 kWh (48 per cent more) – though their water usage is the same.

Buy one to suit your family size and eating habits. If you aren't using it at least four or five times a week, it's too big.

Check the energy label – nowadays they are pretty well all A-rated for energy efficiency, but there's some variation in their washing and drying efficiencies.

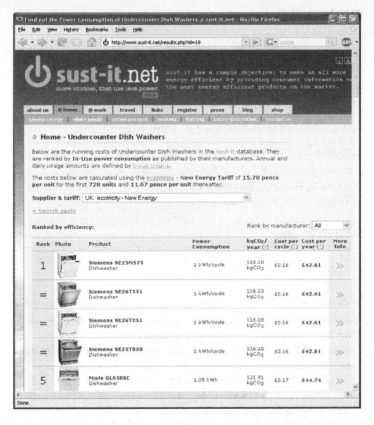

figure 3.1 Sust-it runs a database of energy use of household appliances (**www.sust-it.net**). Use it to check the efficiency of different models when you are thinking of buying a new one.

Fridges and freezers

Fridges and freezers are essentially insulated boxes that work best when full and unopened. The problem is that air moves of its own accord. Open the door and half a fridgeful of cold air falls onto the floor and is replaced with warm air from the room. If the fridge is largely empty, then a lot of cold escapes whenever the door is opened. If it is full then the cold loss will be reduced. Depending upon the size of the fridge, and the state of its occupancy, for every minute that the door is open, it can take three to five minutes' running to restore the internal temperature.

Upright freezers suffer from the same problem – and the energy costs can be higher because the temperature inside has to be brought down so much lower. Internal doors to the shelves, or drawers instead of shelves can help to reduce cold loss. Chest freezers are better in this respect, as the heavy, cold air will stay in place when the lid is lifted, though some will be displaced while you are digging down to the bottom for that emergency loaf you know is down there somewhere.

Fridges and freezers have a very long useful life. Their motors seem to go on indefinitely; door seals may deteriorate over time, but can usually be replaced easily enough; and the cabinets and doors should last forever as long as they are not physically damaged – the inner skin is often quite thin.

Worth doing

- If you have a separate fridge, does it need to be in the kitchen? Where is the coolest place in your house or garage? Will the freezer fit there?
- Make sure that there is enough space behind and above the fridge and freezer for circulation of air to carry away heat from the grill.
- Keep the appliance full to reduce cold air loss when the door is opened.
- Get a fridge thermometer and check the temperatures. (Fridges should run at 0–4°C and freezers at –18°C).
- Defrost the freezer regularly, for greatest efficiency.

Buying guide

- Don't buy anything bigger than you need. If the fridge or freezer is not going to be at least two-thirds full (ignoring crumbled newspaper!) most of the time, then you will not be using it efficiently.
- Check the EU energy label. The best have A+ or even A++ energy efficiency ratings.
- An automatic defrost is worth having. In older designs these can lower the efficiency, so double-check the EU energy label.

A smaller appliance will not necessarily use less energy. The least energy-efficient fridge-freezer on the market at the time of writing was the Whirlpool ARC 2210. This has a fridge capacity of 6.6 cubic feet and a 1.7 cubic feet freezer, but consumes an

figure 3.2 Before buying any household appliances, it's worth paying a visit to the Green Consumer Guide at **www.greenconsumerguide.com**.

estimated 394 kWh per year. Compare this to the current best, the Electrolux ERN29600 with a 7.4 cubic feet fridge and 2.5 cubic feet freezer that uses only 216 kWh per year (figures from **www.sust-it.net**).

Electronic equipment

The main issue with electronic equipment is about unnecessary use of energy, and in particular the standby effect. Video and DVD players, cable tuners, Freeview boxes and other entertainment equipment often do not have off switches, but go into standby mode when not in use, so that they can be fired up again by the remote. In some cases, if you do turn them off at the wall socket, then you may lose current data, e.g. where you had got to in the DVD when you stopped watching. Normally the only effect of turning them off at the mains is that you have to walk across the room to turn them back on again, instead of slumping straight onto the couch and reaching for the remote.

The amount of electricity used by sets during standby is small – but it's continuous. It's worth comparing the total usage when active and when on standby. Take DVD players for example. A reasonably efficient player runs at around 10 watts when active, and 1 watt on standby. As the player will typically be active for perhaps two hours a day, and on standby for 22, you get the following consumption patterns:

Active	10 w × 2 hours =	20 w/hr
Standby	1 w × 22 hours =	22 w/hr
Daily total		42 w/hr

This is using more power when not in use than when it is!

DVD players are something of an extreme case, because they draw very little power in active use. Perhaps a better comparison would be a TV. A typical 30-inch tube TV draws around 100 watts when active, but only 3 watts on standby. Assume that it is in use for four hours a day, and you get these figures:

Active	100 w × 4 hours =	400 w/hr
Standby	3 w × 20 hours =	60 w/hr
Daily total		460 w/hr

60 w/hr over a whole day does not sound much, but it would power an energy-efficient light bulb for over five hours. If we all turned off our equipment properly after use, the cumulative effect nationally would be significant.

With TVs, hifi systems, DVD players, computers and similar electronic equipment, one of the interesting things is how much variation there is in their efficiency. You might think, for instance, that a 32-inch TV would use much the same amount of energy, whoever makes it, but you would be wrong. There is a huge difference between the best and the worst, at least among those with LCD screens – the most efficient, the Loewe Xelos, uses only 75 watts an hour compared to the Samsung equivalent which uses 275 watts – over three times as much. Perhaps this is the new technology effect – LCD screens are recent developments – because there is rather less variation with the cathode ray tube sets. The best of these, from Philips, uses 109 watts an hour, while the least efficient, from Beko, burns only 50 per cent more at 165 watts.

The same variation is also visible in standby modes. Take DVD/video players: JVC machines typically drop to 1 watt on standby, but Toshiba players – which use exactly the same when active – drop only 4 watts.

No-brainer

- Turn equipment off at the mains after use. When buying new, look for models that have an off switch on the box.
- Check out the energy use of any equipment before buying, and aim for the most efficient. You can find the figures for most types and models at Sust-it (**www.sust-it.net**).

Computers ...

In the early days of personal computers, there was a theory that it was better to leave the machine on, in sleep mode, than to turn it off, because the temperature changes when powering up and down tended to stress the soldered joints and the chips. If that was the case – and it was never proved – it certainly is not so nowadays. Modern machines power down almost completely when they go into sleep mode, and it doesn't do them any harm.

The energy demands of PCs varies considerably. The greenest is the Tranquil PC, which consumes under 30 watts (standby 2 watts); the worst currently is the Dell Dimension 9200 which uses 257 watts when fully active, 211 watts in its so-called 'idle' mode, but only 2.2 watts on standby. And this is just the box. Monitors use anything from 20 to 60 watts (17-inch LCD).

Worth doing

- Do a full shut down and turn off the power unless you are coming back to the PC shortly.
- When buying a new PC, make power consumption one of the key considerations – check them out at **www.sust-it.net**.

- If you are involved with a business or other organization that is planning to upgrade its PCs and will have old ones to dispose of, Computers for Charity will put them to good use (they won't collect single PCs). Contact them via their website at **www.computersforcharities.co.uk**.

... and printers

The main issue with printers is not the energy they use – which is not much – but the resources that go into ink and toner cartridges. It takes over a litre of oil (and some aluminium and steel) to manufacture a laser printer cartridge, and around half that to make an ink jet cartridge. Though almost all are refillable, most are used only once before they head for landfill. Current estimates are that over 40 million laser printer cartridges are sold in Europe each year, of which almost 75 per cent are used only once; for ink jet cartridges the figures are nearly 50 million a year with an 80 per cent throw-away rate. The UK has one of the worst recycling rates in Europe for cartridges, with perhaps 10,000 tonnes of them sent to landfill each year.

Printer manufacturers do not encourage refilling, simply because so much of their profit comes from the sale of cartridges – printers are routinely sold below cost, or at very low profit levels, to create a market for their cartridges. Some have even built chips into the cartridge to prevent them from being refilled – the chip must be reprogrammed or replaced, along with the toner. Things will change, eventually, as the WEE (Waste Electrical and Electronic) directive finally came into force last year, and this requires manufacturers to take responsibility for the disposal of their products. In the meantime, it's up to us to save the planet.

No-brainer

Recycle your old cartridges. Remanufacturers will pay for them, giving the money either to you or to a charity. Many cartridges come with envelopes that you can use to post the cartridge to the remanufacturers – Tommy's the baby charity is very active in this area and makes over £50,000 a year through cartridge recycling. If you don't get an envelope, go online to Environmental Business Products Ltd, who will supply envelopes and donate to the charity of your choice.

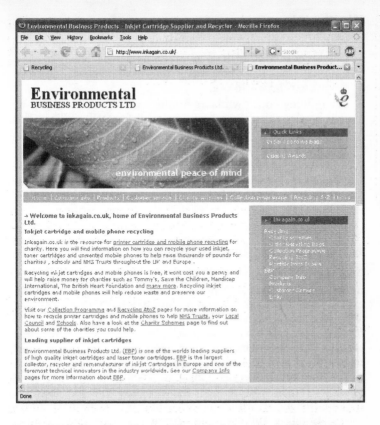

figure 3.3 Environmental Business Products Ltd are the leading charity-oriented remanufacturers in the UK. Find them at **www.inkagain.co.uk**

If you have a steady stream of used cartridges to dispose of in your work, or you are looking for a new source of revenue for your school or club, there are businesses that will pay you directly for them. Values range from 5p to £2.50 each, depending upon their type and whether they have already been refilled, but if you have enough cartridges coming in, it may be worth the effort of organizing it. Two firms to talk to are Cartridge Express at **www.cartridgeexpress.net** and Cash for Cartridges at **www.cashforcartridges.co.uk**.

Worth doing

- Have your old cartridges refilled at Cartridge World. It will usually cost around half as much as a new one. This is a national franchised business – find your nearest branch at **www.cartridgeworld.org**.
- Try refilling your own laser printer cartridges. Toner Top-up sells bottles of toner, and refilling tools for DIY refilling. This is an experiment worth trying – if it doesn't work properly, you will have lost less than the cost of a new cartridge, and if it's OK, you'll save money and the environment. On average you can refill a cartridge three times before one of its moving components wears out. Find out more at **www.tonertopup. co.uk**.

How much electricity are you using?

And that's 'how much right now'? If you have an electricity usage monitor or energy meter (the names vary) you can see exactly how much energy you are using, while you are using it. Why would you want to know? Mainly because it gets you to focus on the question of how much electricity you actually need to use. With a monitor in your hand, you will find yourself irresistibly drawn to walking round the house turning things on to see how much they use, then off – and leaving them off if possible. People who fit them typically find that they save the cost of the meter within months, and go on to have lower electricity bills – and carbon footprint – because they have got into the habit of turning things off.

There are several monitors on the market at present; two worth investigating are:

- Efergy home CO_2 meter from Sust-it at **www.sust-it.net**.
- The Owl electricity monitor from Let's Automate at **www.letsautomate.com**.

They are both around £50 and very similar in design. Each has two components: a device which fits around the mains supply, measures the current flow and transmits that data; and a hand-held receiver which displays the flow in terms of electricity use, CO_2 emissions or money, so that you can see how much of any of them you are using/wasting. Fitting is simple – you just clip the sensor around the mains wire between the electricity meter and the fuse box, stick batteries into the hand-held unit and that's it. The only catch is that the sensor/transmitter unit needs power, so you'll need a socket within reach.

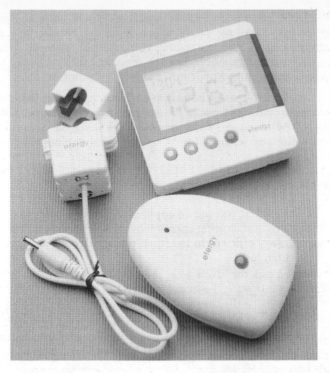

figure 3.4 The Efergy power meter – a simple and effective way to increase your awareness of your energy use, and to reduce wastage. The meter has a memory function so that you can see your usage – and the reductions you are making – over time. Photo courtesy of Sust-it.

Disposal and recycling

All appliances reach the end of their useful life sometime. And then what? With white goods – fridges, cookers, washing machines and the like – there is usually a very simple answer. Most retailers now will remove an old machine when they deliver a new one, and they will send it on for recycling. If this is not an option, your local council-run recycling centre will take them, and if you cannot get them there yourself, councils normally offer a collection service for bulky goods. Recycling fridges and freezers actually costs money – recovering the refrigerant gases is a specialized job – but the sheet metal in white goods gives them some scrap value.

TVs, DVD players and other electronic goods tend to have shorter lives, and are rarely worth repairing nowadays – it's often cheaper to buy new than have equipment repaired. When you do replace appliances, ask the retailer if they will take the old one, and if not, drop it into the local recycling centre.

If an appliance – white goods or electronics – is still working, look for ways to extend its life. Is there a Freecycle group (see page 77) in your area? Contact your local Social Services to see if they have any schemes for reusing working appliances.

Summary

- The longer that you use an appliance, the more value you get from its manufacturing energy – but if new models are much more energy-efficient in use, then replace the old one sooner rather than later.
- Always read the EU energy label, and look for the most energy- (and water-) efficient models.
- The Sust-it database carries energy and cost data on almost all electrical appliances currently on sale (**www.sust-it.net**).
- Most of the energy use in washing machines goes into heating water. Modern ones, with suitable powders or tablets, give just as good results at 30° – and use less energy.
- Fridges and freezers work best when full – even if the space is just filled with crumbled paper.
- Leaving electrical equipment on standby may not use much power, but it is using it pointlessly. Turn off completely after use.
- Printer cartridges should be recycled. Have cartridges refilled if you can, and if not choose remanufactured ones.
- An energy monitor will tell you how much electricity you are using.

04

in the home

In this chapter you will learn:
- about the need to conserve water
- how to freshen the air naturally
- about natural cleaning products
- how to avoid pollutants in paints
- about the environmentally friendly options for furniture and flooring.

In Chapter 02, we looked at the use of energy in the home, and that reducing must be the first priority in making our homes greener places, but there are other issues. We need to look at the chemicals that we use to clean our houses, and ourselves; at the resources that go into our furniture and decorations – and at how and where they are manufactured; and at our water use. Let's start there, because there are some simple decisions and easy savings to be made.

Water use

The issues with water are primarily about limited resources and energy use. Here in the UK we have more than enough rainfall in total to meet our current needs, but not necessarily in the right place or at the right time, and on past trends our needs will rise in the future. The rain falls mainly in the north west while the bulk of the population, and much of the industrial and agricultural demand, is located in the south east. In recent summers, large parts of the south east have seen hosepipe bans and other restrictions on the use of water. Such restrictions will become wider, deeper, more long-lasting and more frequent as the population grows, unless we learn to use water more wisely. (The water companies also need to invest a lot more in the supply system, but that's another matter.)

Even if there was an endless supply of water in the pipes, we should still minimize our usage because of the energy costs. It takes energy to filter, purify and pump water from rivers or underground sources to our homes, and to run the treatment plants to clean waste water before it is returned to the environment. Overall, the water industry uses 2 per cent of the total energy consumed in the UK, and is responsible for 1 per cent of the CO_2 emissions. When you waste water, you also waste energy, and add to greenhouse gases.

No-brainer

- Try not to let a tap run, unused, straight down the plughole. Turn it off while you are brushing your teeth. If you want a small quantity of hot water, heat it in the kettle rather than running a bucketful away waiting for it to run warm.
- When you do have to run the tap to get hot water, you might collect that run-off for watering plants in the garden or on the patio.

- If you are a gardener, fit a water butt to a downpipe and collect rainwater. If your tap water is hard, some plants, especially heathers and azaleas, will appreciate the softness of rainwater.
- Showers normally use less water than baths, though the difference is less marked with power showers. If the shower is in the bath, put the plug in next time, and see how much water you do use!
- Fix dripping taps. Installing a new washer is normally a simple DIY job.

Worth doing

- If you haven't already got one, have a water meter installed. There is nothing like knowing that you are paying by the litre to make you use less water. People typically reduce their water consumption between 5 per cent and 15 per cent after fitting a meter, which is good for the environment, but they also normally find that they pay less on a meter than they did when paying on the rates. Water companies will fit meters, on request, without charge, and they all give you the option of switching back to unmetered water, if you choose to during the first year. It's got to be worth a try.
- Install a low-flush or dual-flush toilet. Over 30 per cent of the water used in most homes goes straight down the loo. A low-flush toilet will reduce this to under 25 per cent. Existing toilets can be fitted with low/dual flush mechanisms, or you can just put a brick in the cistern – that often does the job.
- Taps with aerators use up to 50 per cent less water when things are being washed beneath a running tap. You may be able to fit aerators into existing taps.
- Fit a water-saving head into the shower.
- When watering patio plants or flower beds, a watering can may be more bother, but it puts water only where it is most needed, and you will use significantly less.

Invest in the future

When you are buying a new washing machine or dishwasher, look for the ones which are most water efficient. The EU Energy Label (see page 46) will tell you how much water they use. The Sust-it database at **www.sust-it.net** (page 49) also includes water usage figures.

Cleaning

The issues here are about the impact of cleaning products on the environment and on our health. Is it sensible to spray toxic compounds onto our kitchen work surfaces, into our washing bowls, into the air and onto ourselves in the name of 'cleanliness'?

Fresh air

According to the US Environmental Protection Agency, the levels of pollutants can be from 2 to 100 times higher inside a home than outdoors. The pollutants are mainly VOCs (volatile organic compounds) and they evaporate off from new furniture and carpets and from decorating materials – with the levels declining steadily over a period of months – but also from cleaning products, and in 'air fresheners' (note the quotation marks).

Air fresheners are a particular cause for concern. Manufacturers do test the chemicals used in them, and in recommended use the concentration of those chemicals in the air will be well within recommended safety guidelines, but the question is how little is safe? In 2004, the University of Bristol published the results of a long-term study that showed that in homes where air fresheners were used every day, 32 per cent more babies suffered from diarrhoea, and more had earache, than in those where they were used once a week or less. And it's not just babies who are affected. An earlier study, published in *New Scientist* found that people who used air fresheners were 25 per cent more likely to suffer from headaches, and in 2007, the European Community Respiratory Health Survey showed that the use of cleaning sprays and air fresheners increased the risk of asthma by between 30 per cent and 50 per cent.

The petrochemicals and synthetic scents used in air fresheners cause considerable concern, but where the ingredients are purely natural, this does not necessarily make them safe. Terpenes are chemicals found in citrus oils. They are not harmful when released into the air, but they can react with ozone. In the home and offices, this is produced by printers and photocopies. There are even special 'air purifiers' that generate ozone, which is supposed to improve air quality. Terpenes and ozone combine to form formaldehyde, a respiratory irritant and a known carcinogen.

No-brainer

- Open the windows and let some fresh air in to drive out the smells.
- Bring flowers in from the garden, or buy them – just not those that are flown in from Kenya – and enjoy their scents.
- Keep house plants – broad-leaved ones are best. They help to filter the air. And if they have fragrant flowers, that's a bonus.
- Baking soda will absorb odours from the air and also from carpets and furniture – see page 67.

Household cleaners

Household cleaners can be very nasty products. There are some very potent chemicals out there on the shelves – especially in the products designed for the worst jobs. Check out the labels on drain cleaners, oven cleaners or lavatory cleaners. The ingredient list – if present (and they don't have to tell you what's in them) – may not make much sense, but notice the safety warnings: wear rubber gloves, avoid breathing the fumes, don't get it in your eyes, keep away from children, dispose of empty containers safely. Around 2 per cent of hospital admissions are the direct result of exposure to household cleaners, and the long-term damage to health is something that we are only now starting to understand – a recent EC health study found that furniture sprays and glass cleaners also contribute to the risk of asthma. Do you really want this stuff in your home?

To be *absolutely* sure that the cleaners that you use, in the combinations that you use them, are *absolutely* safe for you, your family or the environment, you can either:

- get a degree in chemistry and another in toxicology, or
- use only the simplest, most basic products.

The former of these options may not be possible for most of us, but the latter *is*, and we will come back to it. If you don't need absolutes, then life is a little more manageable.

No-brainer

Choose eco-friendly products from environmentally-aware firms. You have to watch out for 'greenwashing' here – there are firms which will claim that their products are environmentally friendly, but there is nothing to stop them making these claims (though they may run foul of the Advertising Standards Authority). If you want to be sure that the product is truly eco-friendly, look for the EU Eco-label. Anything which carries this has been tested and assessed, and meets very stringent environmental criteria.

At the time of writing, only these Eco-labelled cleaning products were on sale in the UK:

- **Bunzl Greenline Plus:** household cleaners, bulk sales only – order online at **www.bunzlchs.com**
- **Delphis EcoL:** household cleaners   – order online at **www.delphisindustries.org**
- **Green Tree:** household cleaners, washing-up liquid, washing powder/tablets – buy in store at Robert Dyas or online at **www.the-greentree.com**
- **Sainsbury's Cleanhome:** household cleaners, washing-up liquid, washing powder/tablets, dishwasher tablets – buy in store, or online at **www.sainsburys.co.uk**
- **Simply:** washing powder/tablets, dishwasher tablets – order online at **www.simply-laundry.co.uk.**

figure 4.1 You can read more about the Eco-label and pick up a product guide, with a full list of approved products, at **www.defra.gov.uk/ environment/consumerprod/ecolabel/.**

Just because a firm does not (yet) have an Eco-label for its products does not mean that they are not environmentally friendly. There are some well-established companies with a long track record and a lot of satisfied customers. Here are some key ones to look out for:

- **Ecover** are one of the oldest and largest of the green cleaning businesses. They sell through the high street – you'll find their products in every supermarket and many smaller shops – and they use their website mainly for advertising and information, giving full ingredient lists for all their products.

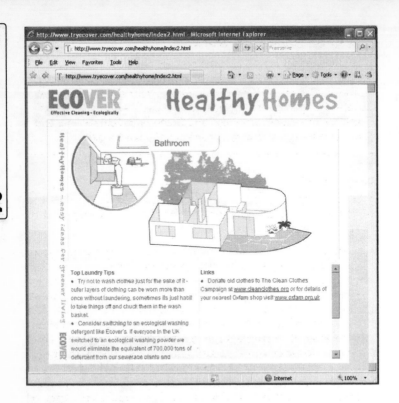

figure 4.2 Visit Ecover at **www.ecover.com**. At the opening screen, point at your country in the list and click on the language to get into the site. Take the tour around their 'house' for tips on greener living.

- **Simple Green** have been supplying eco-friendly cleaning products for 30 years. Based in the US, they are now selling in the UK through their website at **www.simplegreen.co.uk**.
- **Cleen Green** are a small family firm based in the Midlands. They claim to be more driven by ethical and environmental consideration than by the desire to make money, and their prices reflect this. Their general household cleaner, for example, currently retails at £2.60 a litre. Similar products at other green suppliers can be up to £10. They offer a free delivery service around their Nuneaton base, and mail order beyond that. Visit them at **www.cleengreen.co.uk** (and note the spelling of 'cleen').

Do green cleaners work?

The short answer is 'yes'. Environmentally safe cleaners can be as effective, or more effective, than standard commercial products. A survey carried out by Which? magazine in 2007 asked consumers to rate cleaners by performance, ease of use and value for money – and the top scorer was Fresh and Green Bathroom Cleaner and Limescale Remover (buy this online at **shop.wwf.org.uk**).

Worth doing

Instead of buying commercial products, try using these natural substances for cleaning. They are non-toxic, bio-degradable, cheap, and effective!

- **Vinegar** – (preferably distilled, white vinegar). It is a mild acid, but strong enough to cut through grease, limescale and other types of dirt and stains. Vinegar can be used in a whole range of cleaning applications. Here are just a few. Apply it neat on a dry or damp soft cloth to clean water marks off stainless steel pans and sinks. Grass stains can be removed from clothes by soaking them overnight in vinegar. Add a cupful to a bowl of water to clean windows and mirrors. Mix one part vinegar to three parts olive oil to create a wood polish. To shift heavy limescale off taps, wrap them in a cloth soaked in vinegar and leave for a few hours. For more, download *Great uses of Vinegar* from TipKing at **www.vinegarbook.net**.
- **Lemon juice** – This is a stronger acid than vinegar, and can be used to tackle more stubborn stains, in place of bleach. It can also be used to disinfect chopping boards and kitchen surfaces – but do be careful around marble – it will eat into the surface. The one big reservation about the use of lemons is that they all have to be imported, while vinegar can be produced from home-grown barley.
- **Baking soda** – (also known as Bicarbonate of soda or sodium bicarbonate). Another highly adaptable cleaner, with many uses. It is a mild abrasive, and can be mixed to a thick paste with water for scrubbing heavily stained surfaces. Mixed with vinegar it can be used for cleaning bathtubs, sinks or other areas where grease, soap scum and/or limescale are a problem. Mixed with vinegar and diluted with water it makes a good all-purpose household cleaner. It also has the useful property of absorbing smells. A small bowl in the fridge will help to keep it smelling sweet; two or three bowls will freshen the air in a room; sprinkle it into the carpet or onto furniture,

leave it for a while then vacuum up to remove pet smells. And there are lots more uses – check out TipKing's *Baking Soda Book* at **www.bakingsodabook.co.uk**.

- **Elbow grease** – A much under-rated resource. Sometimes all that's needed is water, a suitable brush and a bit of effort.

Vinegar, lemon juice and elbow grease are, of course, fully renewable resources. Bicarbonate of soda is naturally occurring, but also manufactured in great quantities. It is not a scarce resource.

Ecoballs® are an alternative to soaps or detergents for washing clothes. They contain mineral salts which ionize the water, lowering surface tension so that it can penetrate deeper into fabrics. The balls are around £30 for a set of three, but will remain active for several hundred washes until the salt pellets finally dissolve completely – and they can then be refilled. Because there is no detergent present, less rinsing is needed, so a shorter wash cycle can be used. You won't need fabric conditioners either. All in all, they offer significant energy and environmental advantages. The only catch is that they don't cope with stains very well, so you will need to pre-treat stained clothes (with vinegar?).

figure 4.3a

figure 4.3b Ecoballs®, the greenest washing solution: a set of three, flying into action (left) and while refilling the mineral salt pellets (right). Find out more at **www.ecozone.co.uk**. Photos courtesy of Ecozone (UK) Ltd.

But what about all those bacteria?

The question here is, do you need to use antibacterial soaps and kitchen cleaners to ensure that hands and surfaces are free from bacteria? And the answer is, no you do not. Research shows that normal soap and water do the job just as well. There is also a danger that the overuse of antibacterial chemicals may result in more resistant strains.

Cleaning materials

There's a disposable culture in cleaning materials and it needs to change. Paper towels, even those made of recycled paper, represent a waste of resources and energy. You have to throw them away after use – they are not welcome in the recycle bin. And paper towels are not the only disposable cleaners. There are disposable dusters, toilet brushes, mops and cloths, some impregnated with polish or cleaning fluid, and sold on the promise that you can do it with one wipe. They are convenient, most are at least as effective as their reusable alternatives, and – probably the biggest selling point – you don't have to deal with a filthy mop/brush/cloth/bucketful of water when you are done.

Must-do

If you have any disposable cleaning materials, use them – no point in wasting what you already have – then dispose of them, and don't get any more.

Worth doing

• Microfibre cloths are a long-life, reusable, machine-washable alternative to disposable wipes on the one hand and traditional cotton cloths on the other. Used dry, or wet – and without any additional cleaning products – they can pick up both loose dust and dried-on dirt from surfaces. The trick, apparently, is in the microscopic size of the fibres which enables them to lift and retain dirt particles more effectively than cloths made with normal fibres.

• Natural sponges are a greener alternative to artificial sponges (which are made from petroleum derivatives), and work just as well. When they reach the end of their life, they can be composted.

Household waste

Household waste has been a growing problem for a long time, but with growing awareness of the environmental and energy costs of waste and – probably more to the point – the rising cost of landfill, there is pressure on to reduce the amount we put into our bins. Local councils, whose job it is to deal with the waste, have tackled the problem from the disposal end – setting up systems to encourage recycling. Most councils now supply householders with one or more additional bins for recyclable material, and we should make full use of these.

The following materials are all readily recyclable. If, for any reason, your council does not collect any of them, bag them up and drop them in at your nearest recycling centre when you are passing:

- glass
- paper and cardboard, though not waxed or coated cardboard drinks containers
- plastic bottles
- food/drink cans and aluminium trays
- textiles

In theory all types of plastic are recyclable, but there are many different types and they must be separated before processing. At the moment, collection and separation costs outweigh the material value apart from plastic bottles.

As householders we also tackle the problem from the other end, and produce less waste.

- Do not buy disposable cleaning products.
- Avoid over-packaged products.
- Buy in bulk, and in recyclable containers.

We will come back to waste and recycling several times through this book, and have another go at our bins when we turn to food in the next chapter.

Paints and varnishes

There are three environmental issues with paints and varnishes. The first takes us back to where we started this chapter – VOCs (volatile organic compounds); the second relates to disposal of the finishes and of any solvents used with them; the third is about the use of scarce resources.

VOCs in finishes

All standard paints and varnishes, even water-based ones, release volatile organic compounds (VOCs) – mostly during the initial drying phases, but continuing at a lower level for some long while after that. The levels vary immensely, and can be worryingly high. Fortunately, it is usually possibly to tell what the level will be, and to avoid the worst. Most paints and varnishes now carry a VOC label. There is no fixed standard for these, but they tend to follow the design shown here.

There are four levels:

Minimal – 0 to 0.29 per cent
Low – 0.30 per cent to 7.99 per cent
Medium – 8 per cent to 24.99 per cent
High – 25 per cent to 50 per cent

If 'High' on the label isn't enough for you, then read the safety warnings that you'll find elsewhere on the tin. High VOC paints and varnishes contain some quite noxious substances.

No-brainer

Avoid high and medium VOC finishes if at all possible – there are suitable low or medium VOC, water-based alternatives for most applications (see below).

Disposing of paints and solvents

Oil and solvent-based paints, and the white spirit or other solvents used to clean brushes, all count as hazardous substances and must be disposed of carefully. You shouldn't pour any of this stuff down the drain! Small quantities can be put into the domestic waste (sealed in plastic containers). Larger recycling centres often have paint collection points; or your council may collect it on request. Contact your council to find your local arrangements.

But of course, what we are talking about here is disposing of paints bought in the past, because the water-based paints that you will be using in future do not present the same problems. The one disposal issue which you may have is when you have almost full tins of good new paint – those where you realized that the colour was wrong after the first four brushstrokes (we all do it). These are not waste to be disposed of, but resources to be recycled. Again, contact your council to see if they have a scheme for using good paint.

No-brainer
Reduce your disposal problems by only buying what you need. One litre of good quality emulsion paint will cover 6 square metres of wall with two coats – or 4 square metres if you need an extra coat to cope with bare plaster or a major colour change.

A litre of gloss paint will cover slightly less (around 5 square metres), but varnishes go further (up to 8 square metres).

Natural alternatives

Vinyl and acrylic paints and varnishes are petroleum products, and we need to reduce our use of these. Are there any alternatives? Fortunately, yes.

- Clay paints are 100 per cent environmentally friendly – water-based, solvent-free, and containing only natural materials (mainly clay, as you might expect). Clay paint can be used in place of emulsion for walls and ceilings in living rooms and bedrooms. Where a tougher surface is required, the walls can be polished after painting, to give a harder, shinier surface (hard work, but the effects can be stunning). The colours tend to be limited, but attractive. The range from *Terrafino*, one of the leaders in this market, consists of white, ochre, orange, red, brown and grey, but with each colour you can have anything from off-white to full strength. Have a look for yourself at **www.tierrafino.com**.
- Natural emulsions, such as those in the Aquamarijn range, use linseed and other vegetable oils as binding agents, and minerals as the pigments and fillers. The resulting finish is as washable as any ordinary emulsion. For more about these and other eco-friendly paints, visit Construction Resources at **www.constructionresources.com**.
- Gloss paints and varnishes can be made with plant oils – they all used to be until the last century! Thinners, for diluting paint or for cleaning brushes, can also be made from natural products such as citrus oil.

Prices vary for natural paints and varnishes, probably as much as they do for standard products – some of the more specialized ones are very expensive, but clay paints and natural emulsions are comparable in price to good quality acrylics.

figure 4.4 EarthBorn paints are the leading UK manufacturer of natural paints, and the only one to hold the Ecolabel Flower for environmental safety. They offer a full range of finishes for walls, ceilings and woodwork, indoors and out – and with a good selection of colours. See for yourself at **www.earthbornpaints.co.uk**.

Furniture

There was a time when furniture was built to last, and was handed down from generation to generation. In this last half century or so, we have become a throwaway society – we buy cheap then throw things away when they break or become tatty. This is not an ethical, environmentally friendly, resource-conscious way to do things. With furniture, as with so many things, the three Rs apply – we must learn to reduce, reuse and recycle.

Invest in the future

When buying new, buy to last. If it costs twice as much, but will last three or four times as long, so it's better value for you as well as being better use of resources.

Must-do

As far as possible, buy furniture and fittings made from recyclable or renewable materials.

You should only buy **wooden** furniture if it is made from reclaimed timber – which can be of better quality, texture and colour than new timber – or if it is grown in properly-managed forests. Timber from certified sustainable sources carries a label. There are several of these, from different certification schemes, including those for new and recycled timber from the Forest Stewardship Council (FSC).

Why only timber from managed forests?

There are two main reasons. First, in a managed forest, new trees are planted as mature ones are felled, so that future supplies are assured and so that the carbon balance is maintained. Second, deforestation of tropical rainforests through uncontrolled logging is a major problem – it contributes very significantly to CO_2 emissions, as well as destroying irreplaceable eco-systems. Uncertified timber, especially hardwoods, may well come from these sources. This is a real problem – something like a quarter of timber arriving into the UK has been produced illegally. Make sure you are not part of it.

figure 4.5 The Forest Stewardship Council's new and recycled timber labels.

There can be ethical problems with **leather**. Clearly most vegans and vegetarians won't be buying leather furniture, but there are reasons why we should all think twice. The arguments about resource use that apply to meat production also apply to leather – it's just another part of the animal. The other thing to note is that tanning can be highly polluting. The most widely used method is based on the use of chrome, but also uses sulphides, formaldehyde, amongst other toxic chemicals, and consumes over 10,000 gallons of water for every tonne of leather. In the developed world, tough environmental controls are in place to combat this pollution, but elsewhere tanning can be a major environmental and health problem.

Stainless steel is one thing that you can be fairly relaxed about. It is 100 per cent recyclable – and in fact, most of the stainless steel on the market today consists of 50 per cent recycled material. It is also extremely long-lasting, durable and very low maintenance – you will not need to use solvent cleaners or apply high VOC paint or varnish to it to keep it looking good.

Worth doing

Next time you need furniture, consider buying second-hand. (If you like, think of it as young antique, rather than second-hand). It will extend the life of the item, and reduce the need for new ones to be made. Old foam-filled furniture is to be avoided – it can be a real fire hazard – but older, horse-hair stuffed chairs and sofas can be a real find, and well worth the cost of having them reupholstered.

And, of course, rather than junk your old furniture when you do need to get rid of it, put it up for sale, or donate it to one of the charity shops that handles furniture. Or freecycle it! (See the boxed item.)

Freecycle

Freecycle is a worldwide collection of over 4,000 local networks with more than 4 million members. Its philosophy is simple – they are trying to change the world, one gift at a time. If you have something that you no longer want or need, instead of throwing it away, you give it away.

The organization operates through a central website which provides support to the network, and which directs interested individuals – that means you – towards their nearest local group. These work through the Yahoo! Groups system. If people have things to give or are looking for some specific help, they post a message on their group's message board. Other members scan the boards and – with any luck – there will be someone who can make good use of the unwanted item. You have to register as a Yahoo! member first (but that's free), and then apply to join the group (also free).

If no other member can put your unwanted item to use, then the group will have information about other local organizations that might be able to take it. Maximizing the life of things is what freecycle's all about – they estimate that globally they keep 300 tonnes of useful stuff out of landfill every day.

figure 4.6 Freecycle is not just about recycling furniture. All manner of things are offered on the messageboards. Find your nearest freecycle group at www.freecycle.org – there is a simple search system, and if that fails, there is a map-based Browse facility.

Floors and floor coverings

What are the greenest options for floor coverings? The answer to that depends upon what the floors are made of:

- Where there are **wooden floorboards,** the greenest covering is no covering. Sand the boards to remove old paint and varnish, if necessary, then seal with natural oils or varnish. Draughts between the boards can cause a problem of heat loss, so fill with strips of wood, filler or papier-mâché stained to match the wood.

- Where a floor covering is needed, there's a good range of natural materials. For carpeting, apart from wool, there are also coir, seagrass, sisal and jute – all good, hard-wearing alternatives (add rugs where softness is needed). If you want wood flooring, choose solid timber or bamboo (from managed forests, of course) in preference to laminates. It is more expensive, but more durable and is fully renewable – but, as with floorboards, seal it with oil or natural varnish.
- In kitchens and bathrooms, or wherever smooth, washable surfaces are needed, consider natural rubber or linoleum (real lino is made from linseed oil, resins, limestone, wood and jute – all natural and either renewable or very plentiful).

Possible suppliers:

- The Alternative Flooring Company at **www.alternative-flooring.co.uk**
- Construction Resources at **constructionresources.com**
- Dalsouple Rubber Flooring at **www.dalsouple.com**
- Upofloor parquet flooring at **www.upofloor.co.uk**

Summary

- Water may be renewable and recyclable, but it is still not to be wasted – energy is required to purify and distribute water to homes, and to remove and clean sewage. Have a water meter installed and buy water-efficient appliances.
- 'Air fresheners' do not freshen air, they pollute it. Open the windows, bring in flowers, or grow houseplants to improve the air quality in your home.
- Cleaning products can be bad for your health and for the environment. Use natural products, or work with the simplest raw materials – vinegar, bicarbonate of soda and lemon.
- Look for the VOC labels on paints and varnishes, and aim for the lowest possible levels – that's your air that the VOCs will be polluting. Clay paints offer an attractive natural alternative to acrylic emulsions.
- Buy furniture that will last, and made from renewable or recyclable materials. Reuse – buy second-hand, and put items back into circulation if you do need to get rid of them.
- Wood makes a good, ethical flooring, but if coverings are needed there's a good range of natural materials to choose from.

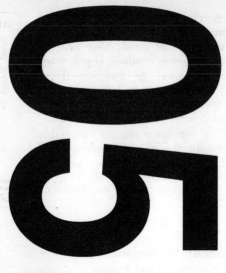

05

food and drink

In this chapter you will learn:
- about fossil fuel energy and food production
- how to reduce your food miles
- about the need for sustainable and ethical fish and meat farming
- how organic foods can be better for you and the environment
- how to reduce food waste, and food packaging
- about the fairtrade movement.

In the UK, as in the rest of the developed world, we live in a time when food is cheap and plentiful, and when just about any type of foodstuff can be bought in the shops at more or less any time of the year. We eat better than kings did 50 years ago! But our eating and drinking habits are not sustainable and not ethical. There are three main issues:

- We are using far too much energy in the production and distribution of food and drink.
- Too many of the people who grow, pick, pack and sell our foods do not get a fair return for their labours.
- We are polluting the environment and ourselves with the chemicals used in growing and processing foods, and with discarded packaging and waste food.

Sometimes these issues overlap. At the time of writing, there is a debate about whether organically grown fruits and vegetables should be labelled 'organic' if they have been flown in from overseas, and also whether or not the ethical consumer should buy them at all – however they are labelled. We'll come back to this later.

Energy and food production

Mechanized farming and the liberal use of artificial fertilizers transformed food production in the twentieth century. A hundred years ago, one farmer could produce enough to feed three other people; now one farmer can feed over 100. But this is only achieved through massive inputs of energy, mainly from oil and gas. Michael Common and Sigrid Stagl in *Ecological Economics* (2005, Cambridge University Press) looked at the energy – human, animal, mechanical and industrial – that went into crop production in pre-industrial and modern farming. They estimated that in peasant farming the ratio of input energy to output energy was over 40:1, but in modern, mechanized agriculture that drops to 1.3:1.

When you focus on protein production, the energy ratios go into the negatives – dramatically so with animal proteins. It takes a little over three units of fossil fuel energy to produce one unit of grain protein (plus carbohydrates), and four units of energy for one of chicken protein, but for beef or lamb protein the ratio shoots up to 50:1. As long as oil has been cheap and plentiful, this has not been a problem, but with rising prices and falling stocks of oil, this is simply not sustainable.

Unless you are a farmer, you cannot change how much energy is put into food production – but you can choose to buy those foodstuffs which take less energy. And that essentially means vegetables rather than meat, and organically grown rather than produced by the agro-chemical industry. We'll come back to both of these issues later.

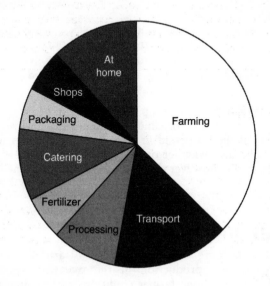

figure 5.1 In 2006, 17 per cent of the UK's CO_2 emissions arose from the food chain. As might be expected, agriculture had the most impact, being responsible for nearly 40 per cent or 45 per cent if the energy used in fertilizer production is included. Transport, at 17 per cent makes up the next biggest slice of the pie.

Methane and meat

The fossil fuel energy that goes into meat production has its impact on global warming – according to research published by New Scientist this year, each 1 kg of meat takes 36 kg CO_2 emissions. But CO_2 is not the only greenhouse gas. Methane, a by-product of the digestive systems of cows and sheep, is also a greenhouse gas, and over 20 times more potent in its effect than CO_2. Organic farming is no help here – organically raised animals release more methane than those reared on conventional foodstuffs.

It is a significant problem. Depending on its feed, a cow will release anything up to 500 litres of methane a day, and the 10 million in the UK are responsible for over one third of the country's methane emissions. Looked at another way, a day's methane output from one cow is equivalent to the CO_2 emissions produced by driving a mid-sized car over 150 miles.

Of course, methane is a fuel. In Sweden they already have a project to produce methane in commercial quantities from cows' guts (from the abattoir). Perhaps one day they'll find a way of capturing it from them while they are going about their daily rumination.

Food miles

Fossil fuel input, of course, only *starts* at the farm. It then continues right down the supply chain, in its processing, packaging, storage and transportation. The distance food travels between the producer and your table is a crucial element in the total energy costs. This is sometimes expressed in 'food miles'. It's a crude measure – distance alone is not the only factor – but it does help to focus on energy costs, and to get people thinking more about local production and consumption.

Air miles

Air miles are the most marked aspect of this – 95 per cent of the fruit and 50 per cent of the vegetables in UK stores are imported. Much of this travels by sea or overland, and only 1 per cent by air – but that 1 per cent is responsible for over 10 per cent of the total food transport CO_2 emissions. And it is a very energy-inefficient way to move materials. It's been estimated that it takes nearly 100 calories of fuel energy to fly in 1 calorie's worth of asparagus from South America; carrots from South Africa compare relatively well at only 66:1, but with regard to iceberg lettuces from the USA, the ratio doubles to 130 calories of fuel to 1 calorie of food. This is not good, and what's more worrying is that air freight has increased significantly, doubling during the 1990s and still rising.

Some of this air-imported food is exotic, but much of it is unseasonal. We fly in French beans from Kenya, tomatoes from Saudi Arabia, apples from South Africa, mushrooms from Zambia, baby sweetcorn from Thailand, asparagus from

Peru – even Brussels sprouts from Australia. These can all be grown here in the UK, or close by in Europe, but only for part of the year.

Road miles

Our food travels a long way nowadays, on its route from the field to the plate. Fifty years ago, most vegetables and much meat would have gone from farmer to the local wholesale market then on to the local shops, perhaps travelling no more than 20 or 30 miles in total. Today, all but a tiny percentage of our food is sold through supermarkets, and that has had a major impact on road miles.

Supermarkets generally prefer to deal with a few large suppliers for any given product. They want guaranteed supplies and products with a good shelf-presence and a long shelf-life – uniform size and blemish-free skin are usually more important than good flavour – and they drive a hard bargain over prices. Small (local) suppliers don't have the economies of scale that will enable them to compete on price, and cannot produce the regular quantities that they need. And those large suppliers are not necessarily in the UK. A more favourable climate (reducing the heating costs of the growing time) and lower wage rates may well outweigh the extra cost of transport, allowing overseas suppliers to deliver their produce at lower prices.

Even where the suppliers are in the same country, supermarkets now collect most of their foods into large regional centres and distribute it out from there to the stores, instead of taking it directly from supplier to store. This has produced not only an increase in miles travelled, but also an increase in the use of the larger HGVs, which have more environmental impact. In the last 30 years, the annual amount of food moved by HGVs has increased by a quarter, and the average length of each trip is up by 50 per cent.

The bulk of our food is now processed to a greater or lesser extent. At one end of the scale there are washed and pre-packed fruit and vegetables, with salad greens and complete salads sold table-ready. At the other end are complete meals, shrink-wrapped, frozen or tinned. There are packaging and food quality issues here, but at this stage the point is that the processing plant is another stop on the travels. Your local-grown watercress or locally made cheese may have travelled 200 miles to the preparation and packaging factory before being sent to the distribution centre and then on to the local store.

But you can't just blame the supermarkets – it's the whole food industry that is responsible, and the EU's Common Agricultural Policy is a major contributor. It distorts the market in such a way that the industry can ship identical produce between countries and make a profit from it. Caroline Lucas, the Green Party MEP, campaigns against this lunacy in her Great Food Swap report. She notes that in 1998, Britain imported 61,400 tonnes of poultry from the Netherlands and exported 33,100 tonnes of poultry to the Netherlands; overall it imported 240,000 tonnes of pork and 125,000 tonnes of lamb and exported 195,000 tonnes of pork and 102,000 tonnes of lamb. The story is the same with milk: in 1997, 126 million litres of liquid milk and 23,000 tonnes of milk powder was imported into the UK and 270 million litres and 153,000 tonnes of powder were exported. (To read more, go to **www.carolinelucasmep.org.uk/publications/greatfoodswap. html**.)

We also have to take some of the blame ourselves. No one forced us to switch to supermarkets for our shopping; we did it from choice. (Or rather, so many of us switched from choice that small local shops have become an endangered species, and there is no practical alternative to the supermarket in too many areas.) And almost all of us drive to the supermarket.

In 2005, the UK government commissioned a report into the *Validity of Food Miles as an Indicator of Sustainable Development*. It found that in 2002, transporting the UK's food took up a quarter of all HGV mileage within the UK and produced 10 million tonnes of CO_2. (It was also responsible for 19 million tonnes of CO_2 emissions in overseas road transport and air freight.) The report found that food transport was also responsible, each year, for over £9 billion of social and environmental costs, including congestion, accidents and infrastructure damage. It noted, 'The rise in food miles has led to increases in the environmental, social and economic burdens associated with transport. These include carbon dioxide emissions, air pollution, congestion, accidents and noise.'

The report made a number of recommendations for how the government and the food industry could start to reduce the costs and impacts of road food transport, but the question for us is – What can we do as consumers? Can we reduce food miles?

The answer of course, is 'yes'. And we can have an impact at two levels.

1 Directly, we can reduce the food miles in our own groceries by changing our buying habits.

2 Indirectly, we can add to the pressure on the government and food industry to change their policies and practices – and we can do this through the shopping basket as well as in more active ways.

figure 5.2 The Food Climate Research Network is an excellent source of detailed information on the impact of food on climate change. Visit them at **www.fcrn.org.uk**.

It's not just about fuel and CO$_2$

Longer journeys mean more time in transit. Fruit and vegetables lose their freshness, their flavour and their vitamin content the longer they spend on the road. Transporting live animals raises ethical questions whatever the distance, but longer journeys can only add to their distress.

How can I reduce my food miles?

No-brainer

Use your small high street shops

Use your local greengrocers or butchers if you are lucky enough to have them. Small shops will normally get their supplies from the local wholesale market, which is where local growers sell their produce. And you won't just lower your food miles doing this, you will also:

- reduce packaging waste, as greengrocers tend to sell more loose and less pre-packed products
- help to keep your high street and its community alive.

On the down side, if you want to buy fairtrade bananas and other imported fruit, you are more likely to find them at the supermarket than at the small greengrocers. We'll come back to fairtrade later.

Buy local-grown food

Whether you are shopping in the supermarket or the greengrocers, check the labels, or ask the shop staff, to find out where the produce was grown, and buy as local as you can. But 'local' has an elastic definition here. Strawberries grown in the same county are to be preferred over those from elsewhere in the UK, which are better than those from mainland Europe, which are better than those from further afield. Some fruits and vegetables have to come from a distance, but sea transport is very energy efficient – it uses less fuel to ship in a box of bananas from the Caribbean than to fly in a box of figs from Greece. Avoid buying anything brought in by air – do you really need Kenyan green beans and Thai baby sweetcorn?

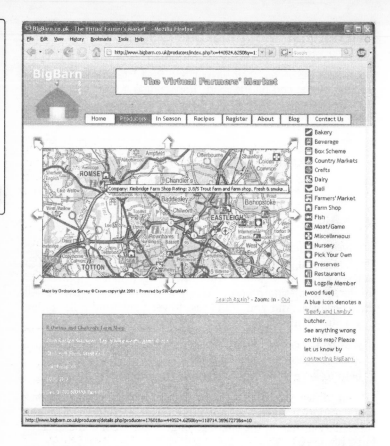

figure 5.3 You can find your local food producers through the web. BigBarn at www.bigbarn.co.uk has a very comprehensive database, and is easy to use – just type in your postcode. BigBarn also features articles and recipes on seasonal food.

Must-do

Eat more seasonal food

Let's get a bit more specific. This is not just about eating what's in season – because any fresh produce must be in season, by definition. This is about eating what's in season in your locality, and we'll be stricter about 'local' here and limit it to the UK, or even to your county.

Eating local seasonal food will obviously reduce your food miles, but it also has other benefits. You will enjoy fruit and vegetables at their best, and at their freshest. It will help to tune you into the natural rhythms of the year. And seasonal food in any case tends to be appropriate for the time of year – salads and soft fruits make lighter meals for the warmth of summer days, while root vegetables and more solid greens give a solid heart to winter food.

You have to think more about your shopping and your diet if you decide that you are going to eat only seasonal foods, and it can be hard to persuade children – or adults – to change their eating habits overnight. If you have a family, work towards seasonal eating.

The following pages provide a month-by-month guide to help you plan your food buying. It includes those foods which are being harvested each month, and which are available from low-tech stores – barns and cellars. The summer fruits and salad vegetable seasons can all be extended another month either way when grown under glass or in polytunnels.

Is hothouse grown okay?

The seasons can be extended further by the use of artificial heat and light, but the energy inputs here tend to knock out the savings in food miles. It's arguable that it takes less energy to transport tomatoes from Spain, where they are grown without heat, than to heat greenhouses in the UK. The ethical solution to this is simple. Don't eat fresh tomatoes outside of the unheated local season.

Season food, month-by-month

	Fruit	Vegetables	Meat	Fish
January	apples, pears, rhubarb (forced)	beetroot, cabbage, carrots, celeriac, Jerusalem artichokes, leeks, parsnip, shallots, sprouts squash, turnips	goose	lobster, scallops
February	apples, pears, rhubarb (forced)	cabbage, carrots, cauliflower, celeriac, chard, chicory, leeks, parsnip, shallots, spinach, sprouts, squash	goose, guinea fowl	halibut, lobster, mussels
March	apples, pears, rhubarb	beetroot, carrots, cauliflower, leeks, purple sprouting broccoli, radishes, sorrel, spring greens		lobster, sardines
April	rhubarb, strawberries	carrots, kale, lettuce, morel mushrooms, radishes, spinach, watercress	spring lamb	cockles
May	cherries, rhubarb	asparagus, broccoli, broad beans, carrots, cauliflower, new potatoes, radishes, rocket, samphire, sorrel, spinach, spring onions, watercress	lamb, duck, wood pigeon	sardines, sea bass, sea trout

June	blackcurrants, cherries, gooseberries, redcurrants, strawberries	asparagus, aubergines, broad beans, broccoli, carrots (new), cauliflower, Chinese leaves, courgettes, fennel, green beans, lettuce, peas, peppers, tomatoes	Welsh lamb	crab, grey mullet, salmon
July	blackcurrants, gooseberries, loganberries, redcurrants, strawberries, tayberries	asparagus, aubergines, broad beans, broccoli, cabbage, cherries, courgettes, cucumber, fennel, french beans, lettuce, peas, peppers, new potatoes, tomatoes, watercress	Welsh lamb	crab, grey mullet, salmon
August	apples, greengages, loganberries, plums, strawberries	aubergines, chard, courgettes, fennel, leeks, lettuce, peas, peppers, new potatoes, sweetcorn	Welsh lamb, hare	skate, john dory, crayfish
September	apples, blackberries, damsons, figs, pears, plums, strawberries	aubergines, beetroot, broccoli, cabbage, cucumber, curly kale, lettuce, marrows, onion, spinach, sprouts, swedes, sweetcorn	autumn lamb, partridge, wood pigeon, venison, grouse	brown trout, oysters, sea bass, mussels

October	apples, elderberries, figs, pears	beetroot, cauliflowers, courgettes, Jerusalem artichokes, leeks, lettuce, marrow, kale, pumpkin, squash, watercress	autumn lamb, grouse, guinea fowl, partridge	oysters, mussels
November	apples, chestnuts, cranberries, quinces, pears	beetroot, cabbage, cauliflower, Jerusalem artichokes, leeks, parsnips, potatoes, pumpkin, sprouts, swede	grouse, goose, wild duck	oysters, mussels
December	apples, pomegranate, pears	beetroot, red cabbage, carrots, celeriac, celery, swedes, Jerusalem artichokes, parsnips, sprouts, turnips	turkey, wild duck, goose	sea bass
All year (fresh or from storage)		mushrooms, onions, potatoes	beef, pork, chicken, duck	cod, farmed salmon, farmed trout

One of the best websites for learning more about seasonal food is Eat the Seasons at **www.eattheseasons.co.uk**. They have a monthly guide to what's in season, with matching recipes, as well as articles on food and links to local and/or organic food producers, retailers and online suppliers.

Worth doing

Farm shops and farmers' markets

It is worth using farm shops and/or farmers' markets if they are in your area. If you have to drive 20 miles out into the countryside or to the next town with a market, then this is probably not a good thing. (Food miles are food miles whether it's the supermarket lorry or your car which is clocking them up.)

There are farmers' markets now throughout the UK, some open every week, others appearing monthly. It's a well-organized and supervised system. On a proper market – one that has the stamp of approval from FARMA (the National Farmers' Retail & Markets Association) – the produce offered for sale must have been 'grown, reared, caught, brewed, pickled, baked, smoked or processed' by the stallholder, who lives and works in the local area. Prices tend to be a little higher than in the high street shops, but it's hard to find fresher fruit and vegetables, and the quality of the meat and other food products is normally very high. If you want to know more about FARMA, head for their website at **www.farmersmarkets.net**.

There are currently over 1,000 FARMA certified farm shops in the UK, selling food grown or reared on the farm. Some of these are pick-your-own farms. Prices tend to be lower here, and of course you can know – to the minute – just how fresh your produce is!

Find out where and when the markets are in your area, and locate your local farm shops. If you have to get into the car to visit them, look for ways to minimize your impact. Can you stock up the freezer, so that you do not have to go so often? Can you shop for your neighbours while you are there, and reduce their food miles?

figure 5.4 To find your nearest farmers' market, go to
www.farmersmarket.net and pick your county or use the postcode search.
Local farm shops can be found in the same way at the sister site
www.farmshopping.net.

Fresh to your door

If it is not convenient or practical for you to visit the local growers, they can come to you. Join a box scheme and have a box of fruit and vegetables delivered to your door each week. These are largely seasonal and mainly locally grown, and some schemes are only organic. It can take a while to get used to these schemes. The amount of control you have over the content will vary, according to the supplier, but it is going to be largely governed by the seasons, and you may have to adjust your eating habits to get the best out of your box. Treat the box as a challenge and an opportunity – what has nature's bounty delivered this week? A box brings you closer to the eating habits of people who grow their own food. You look at what's available and plan your food from there, rather than thinking about what you would like to eat and going to buy the ingredients – which is how supermarkets have encouraged us to be.

The people running these box schemes are mainly small farmers, many of whom already run farm shops or market stalls, and they will only deliver within a few miles of their base – the emphasis is on local sales of local produce. That should not present you with a problem. Box schemes have really taken off in the last few years, so that there are now very few places in the UK that are not within range of one or other deliverer. You can find the schemes running in your area at the *Veg Box Schemes* website (see below).

If there are no small local suppliers in your area, there are a few larger businesses running box schemes, but note that the emphasis here is on organic rather than local. *Riverford Organic Vegetables* (at **www.riverford.co.uk**) supply across the south of England. *Abel & Cole* (at **www.abel-cole.co.uk**), following a recent sell out to a private equity firm, is going nationwide at the time of writing.

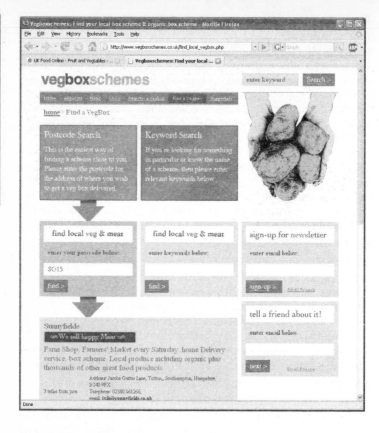

figure 5.5 Find your local suppliers at the veg box scheme website,
www.vegboxschemes.co.uk.

Grow your own

There is nothing quite like the taste of young carrots pulled,
washed, cooked and eaten within half an hour, or cherry
tomatoes eaten straight off the plant. It doesn't require great
effort to enjoy your own produce – and to reduce your food
miles. You can grow:

- herbs on a sunny windowsill
- herbs, tomatoes, peppers, chillies, strawberries, runner beans,
  salad greens and more in pots on a patio or balcony

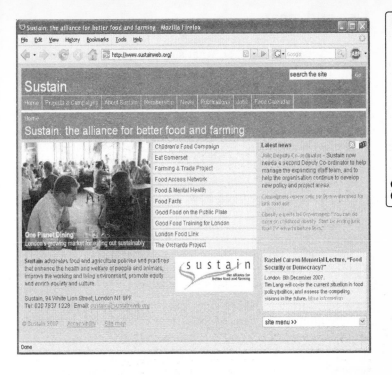

figure 5.6 If you would like to get involved in promoting the use of local foods, visit Sustain, the alliance for better food and farming, at **www.sustainweb.org**.

- beans, peas, purple sprouting broccoli, cabbages (ornamental or green) and other vegetables with attractive foliage or flowers in the flower beds of a small garden – runner beans were originally grown for their flowers
- a rich variety of vegetables, in short rows in a small plot – if stored carefully, seeds will remain good for several years so that you do not need to waste the rest of the packet after sowing your short row.

Fish and meat

'Grow your own' is not a possibility for most of us when it comes to fish and meat. So what should we be looking for?

With fish, the key issue is sustainability. Over-fishing is threatening the existence of many species – scientists estimate that nearly 80 per cent of the world's fish stocks are in danger. In enclosed seas and inland waters, there is a realistic hope of controlling the level of fishing, but with deep-sea fishing, there is far less hope of the sort of international co-operation that would be needed to protect stocks.

Fish farming can be the answer, but it depends upon what sort of fish is being farmed and how. To rear salmon, for example, you need to feed them on a high-protein diet, and much of that currently comes from bottom-trawled fish, i.e. fish caught in nets that are dragged along the seabed, a very destructive type of trawling. So, salmon farming tends to increase over-fishing. Tilapia, on the other hand, is a herbivore and can be fed on plant-based foods and farmed sustainably.

As a general rule, when buying fish, check that it is line-caught – on dolphin-friendly and seabird-friendly lines – or sustainably farmed.

If you really want to do this properly, you also need to take seasons into account, and the times of year when different sorts of fish are in season. The Marine Conservation Society runs the very helpful FishOnLine website at **www.fishonline.org**. They have handy lists of what fish you can eat, and what you should avoid, as well as an extensive purchasing guide that sets out when you can buy different types of fish, and what harvesting methods are acceptable.

With meat, the key issue is probably animal welfare. It's only fair, if you are going to eat an animal, that it should have had a decent quality of life up until the point of slaughter. Factory farming, mainly of poultry, pork and veal, can produce meat at lower prices than free range, but the non-monetary costs are high. The animals live in cramped conditions, on wire mesh or concrete floors, with no chance to do anything much other than eat and grow, and with limited or no interaction with other animals. Chickens need to forage for their food, pigs need to socialize, calves need to suckle their mothers. And we need them to lead contented lives – at a higher level, having respect for other creatures should be one of the things that make a decent human being, and at a lower level, free-range animals that have moved freely and used their muscles taste better.

No-brainer

Buy only free-range chickens (and eggs) and farm-reared, field-raised pork.

Worth doing

Join the campaign against factory farming. Visit **www.factoryfarming.org.uk/** or **www.factoryfarming.com**.

Organic food

The way that we grow food raises some major environmental concerns, ranging from the destruction of the Amazon rain forest to clear space for soya bean cultivation, to nitrate run-off in the waterways, with top soil erosion, the loss of biodiversity and much else in between. As consumers, it is hard for us to have much impact on many of these issues – though we can do more as campaigners – but we can encourage more sustainable, less damaging farming by buying more organic food.

What is organic?

Organic food is grown as naturally as possible, using no artificial fertilizers, herbicides, pesticides or growth hormones. The farming techniques are designed to be sustainable, keeping the soil in good condition, and using the minimum of fossil fuel energy. Animals must be fed on organic foodstuffs, have good living conditions and be spared unnecessary distress in transport and slaughter.

There is no single, absolute definition of 'organic', but in the UK the Soil Association is generally recognized as the leading body, and their accreditation carries most weight.

If food carries the Soil Association's symbol, it means that it has been produced to strict animal welfare and environmental standards. There are a number of aspects to this, and each is carefully defined. For example, to maintain fertility and soil quality, organic farmers will use crop rotation and can apply composts and manure, and certain natural mineral fertilizers. They cannot use artificial fertilizers which lack the trace elements needed for truly healthy crops, and which can inhibit the growth of the microbes that are needed for healthy soil.

Sales of organic food in the UK have boomed over the last few years, alongside the growth of the 'good food' culture and the increased enthusiasm for fitness and personal well being. Though they still account for a relatively small percentage of the total food market, organic food sales rose by 30 per cent in 2006 and have become much more mainstream, with all the supermarket chains now having organic sections. In keeping with the low-impact spirit of organic farming, most supermarkets now source at least part of their organic produce from local growers.

Is organic actually any better?

It's certainly better for the environment. The agriculture industry in the UK uses upwards of 4 billion litres of pesticides each year – organic farming does not use them. Though modern pesticides are not as damaging as DDT, their long-term effects are not known and they are getting into our food chain. With artificial fertilizers, soil quality tends to deteriorate over time so that heavier applications are needed to get the same yields, increasing the energy costs of production and the run-off of nitrates. Organic farming's use of compost, animal manure and 'green manure' (crops grown specifically to capture nitrogen, and then ploughed back in) results in healthier soil where fertility is at least maintained and often rises.

Some organic foods may be better for you than conventionally grown ones. There is some evidence that crops tend to have higher levels of Vitamin C, magnesium and phosphorus (though with all fruit and vegetables, however grown, vitamin levels decline steadily after picking, so fresher, local produce will tend to have higher levels).

UK-grown organic food may well have a better flavour than non-organic, but that may be more to do with the variety that is grown, and the care given to it by its committed grower – organic farmers aren't just in it for the money! This argument may not apply to imported organic fruits and vegetables which tend to come from larger plantations. There is also another argument about organic foodstuffs from overseas, and that is about how it gets here.

Can air-freighted food be organic?

At the time of writing, there has been a vigorous debate about whether organically grown food that is flown in from overseas should be labelled organic. The outcome has been something of a compromise. The Soil Association has decided that air-freighted foodstuffs can carry their organic symbol if they are grown organically and under fairtrade conditions. I think it's a false debate. It doesn't matter whether you can call it 'organic' or not. At present the most pressing issue has to be greenhouse gas emissions and climate change – flying in fresh food is environmentally damaging and unsustainable.

Worth doing

Organic foods are normally more expensive than the conventional alternative, but are free from the herbicide and pesticide residues which may be damaging to us in the long term. Organic farming is, by definition, sustainable, in contrast to conventional agriculture that is dependent upon heavy inputs of energy – primarily from fossil fuels. For our own personal good, and to help ensure future food supplies for us all, we should buy more organic foods.

Do I have to go vegan to be ethical?

Well, if you want to be truly ethical, the answer is probably 'yes'. It certainly ticks all the boxes.

Currently a substantial amount of the world's crops go to animal feed to produce meat for the wealthier countries. If no one ate meat, the world would be able to produce more than enough food to keep everyone well fed.

We noted earlier how much more fossil fuel energy goes into producing meat compared to crops. A meatless diet would reduce fuel use and CO_2 emissions. (And let's not forget the methane emitted by cows and sheep, and its contribution to global warming.)

You don't have to be an animal rights activist to recognize that not all animals are reared, or transported or slaughtered in ideal conditions. If you are a vegan, no animal is suffering on your behalf.

The vegan diet, with its avoidance of all dairy products, is too stringent, and requires too much dedication, for most people. Is vegetarianism an ethically acceptable alternative? Well, whether you look at it from an animal rights/welfare or use of resources angle, the answer has to be 'not quite'. Some meat is a by-product of the dairy industry. If you want milk, your cows must have calves and what are you going to do with the ones that you don't need for the dairy herd? What do you do with your chickens after their egg-laying days are over?

Eating less meat has got to be better for the environment. Ensuring that the meat you do eat is ethically reared and slaughtered is essential. Organic is preferable.

Food waste

There is a very simple issue here. Recent research showed that in the UK, on average, we throw away one third of the food we buy, and that half of this is still fit to eat. This represents not just a waste of money by individuals – an estimated £400 per household, but also a huge waste of resources for society as a whole – 7 million tonnes per year. If we could eliminate most of that waste, we could cut our total CO_2 emissions by 5 per cent or more, take 1 in 10 HGVs off the roads, and save a lot of landfill.

Food waste should not go into landfill because it rots, producing methane, a greenhouse gas, and leachate – toxic liquid that can find its way back into the waterways. Local councils and the food industry are exploring more eco-friendly ways to deal with food waste. Composting is a good use for raw vegetable waste, especially when combined with trimmings, cuttings and other vegetation from parks and gardens; meat and processed foods can be converted to bio-fuel and/or used for electricity generation. These initiatives are to be encouraged. Find out what your local council is doing, and if they aren't doing anything special with food wastes, ask why not. You might like to point them in the direction of Inetec, who develop large-scale waste management systems – visit them at **www.inetec.co.uk** to find out more.

The charity Fareshare runs a community food network that collects unwanted food – surplus, or near or past its 'best before' date – from shops and businesses. It is sorted, and the edible is used in local feeding projects, while the rest is sent for composting or bio-fuel or other forms of recycling. The organization is largely funded by fees for waste removal, but depends upon volunteers to get the jobs done. If you would like to get involved, contact them through the website at **www.fareshare.org.uk**.

Restaurants and food processors produce something like 100,000 tonnes of used cooking oil a year, but this is increasingly recognized as a resource rather than as a disposal problem. It can be purified, refined and converted into animal feed or bio-diesel, or used in the manufacture of soap and cosmetics. A few councils run cooking oil collection services for householders. If this is not available in your area, cooking oil can be added to the compost, but otherwise should go (in a bottle) into the bin.

The professionals waste more

Households may waste a lot of food, but even more is wasted by shops, restaurants, manufacturers and food processors – around 17 million tonnes per year, and 10 per cent of this is fit for consumption.

Reducing your food waste

We can all reduce the amount of food that we throw away, and we can do so very easily. The following suggestions could all be listed as 'no-brainers' – in that there is no question that these are good things to do – but they do require a little thought!

Must-do

- Only buy what you need. Think ahead to the meals that you will be preparing between now and the next shopping trip. Make a list of the ingredients you will need for them, and then stick to that list. If you are tempted by something off the list while you are shopping, then revise your list so that you buy that eye-catcher instead of, rather than as well as, your planned foods.

- Eat before you shop. It's harder to resist impulse buying when you are hungry.
- Avoid value packs and '2 for 1' offers on fresh produce unless you can freeze what you don't need immediately.
- Store fresh food in the fridge, and check that its temperature is 5° or below.
- Keep an eye on the dates. Remember that 'best before' means precisely that. You can eat food after its 'best before' date, but it won't be as good – you might want to cook what would otherwise have been eaten raw, or add a bit more spice to the cooking. 'Use by' *does* mean use by the given date, so plan ahead and make sure that you do.
- Weigh and measure when you are cooking, and keep left-overs to a minimum (though left-overs are rarely a problem for long if you have teenagers in the house).

Worth doing

Raw kitchen waste, including vegetable peelings, outer leaves, skins, tea bags and coffee grounds, and all manner of garden waste – weeds, prunings, grass cuttings and the like – can be turned into compost and used to enrich the soil. You don't even need a garden – there are small, closed systems that you can use indoors. There are two approaches to composting:

Traditional compost heaps

These do need a garden, because you need some space and you need exposed soil. There is a minimum size for effective composting. The heap needs to be half a metre or so in every dimension to generate enough heat in the middle for vegetable matter to break down fully. A simple heap on the ground will eventually turn into compost, but you get much better results, faster, if the waste matter is enclosed in something to keep the rain off and to retain heat which encourages the essential bacterial action. The container can be a bottomless wooden box, with a cover, or a plastic bin with a lid. Worms and other minibeasts will come up from the soil and set to work on your waste, turning all manner of vegetation into a fine, crumbly, rich, dark mixture.

You can build a wooden composter very easily, but check first with your council – many offer plastic bins at big discounts, and they do work very well.

At the simplest, you can just chuck your kitchen and garden waste in the top, then start to shovel compost out of the bottom next year. You will get a better quality of compost, and in a shorter time, if you take a little more care over what goes in and how. There are two broad categories of compostable materials, and you need both in your bin:

- wet, green material such as kitchen waste, plant prunings and grass cuttings which provide nitrogen and rot quickly – a foot-deep layer of cuttings and other soft waste will be reduced to virtually nothing in a few days
- drier fibrous matter such as fallen leaves, paper or cardboard to improve the structure and let the heap breathe, but rot relatively slowly.

If the mix is too wet, it can get so compacted that it festers rather than rotting properly. If it is too dry, then worms cannot live in it – and they are an essential part of the process – and rotting is very slow. To turn pure leaves into leaf mould, for example, takes three years.

A layer of ordinary soil every now and then will also help to balance the mix.

Wormeries

Wormeries are closed containers that rely on the action of worms to turn kitchen waste into compost. Designs vary, but typically there are several layers of trays with mesh bottoms, above a collection tray with a tap. You fill the trays with waste, working from the bottom up. The worms go into the bottom tray, and will munch their way through the waste – eating half their own bodyweight a day – turning it into worm poo, or compost as it is politely known, and liquid fertilizer, which can be added to your watering can. Once they have finished with the bottom tray, the worms migrate to the one above, and the contents of the bottom tray can be added to your flowerpots and vegetable beds – giving spectacular results. The empty tray goes to the top, ready for the new waste.

figure 5.7 If you want to know more about composting, and to find out about low-cost bins, visit the home composting page at recycle now (**www.recyclenow.com/home_composting**).

The process is much faster than traditional composting – you're talking six weeks from waste to compost, not six months – and you can get totally closed containers which are suitable for patios or even indoor use.

figure 5.8 Probably the cheapest wormery on the market, but no less effective, is this two-tray system, with a collector, in recycled plastic from Worm City. Go visit the city and find out more: www.wormcity.co.uk. Photo courtesy of Worm City.

Wormeries do require a bit more care than compost heaps. Because the wormeries are closed systems, the worms are dependent upon you for their survival. Worms are robust and adaptable, but there are limits. If there is not enough food, they will die off; if it gets overheated (don't stand them in full sun in summer), they will die; if it gets too cold (don't leave them exposed to the worst of the elements in winter), they will die. You need to be a little more selective in the waste that you put in. Worms don't like acid foods, so if you are including citrus peels, you will need to add a little lime to neutralize this.

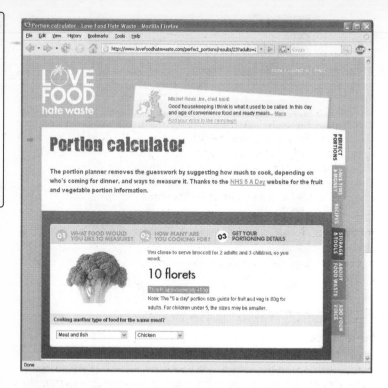

figure 5.9 In late 2007, WRAP launched its Love Food Hate Waste campaign for reducing food waste. Their website has lots of information about the problem, and suggestions for how you can help. Go and see for yourself at **www.lovefoodhatewaste.com**.

Food packaging

The basic problems with food packaging are the waste of resources it causes and its disposal – a third of household waste is food packaging, adding up to a total of over 6 million tonnes a year in the UK, and most of this goes to landfill where it will decay slowly over the next few hundred years. (There is also a cost factor – packaging accounts for an estimated one sixth of the total food bill for the average household.) The key issues are how to reduce the resources that go into packaging and the amount that we throw away.

Supermarkets and their suppliers are the worst culprits. In 2007, the Local Government Association published a report on food packaging. Researchers had bought the same basket of 29 standard foodstuffs – meat, cheese, fruit, vegetables, bread, biscuits, etc. – from different stores and compared the quantity and nature of the packaging. They found that packaging made up 5 per cent, on average, of the total weight of the basket. *Tesco* goods had the least – under 700 grams – while that from *Marks and Spencer*, a firm which prides itself on being greener than the herd, came to nearly 800 grams. If packaging is recyclable, quantity is less of an issue, but only 60 per cent of that from *Marks and Spencer* is recyclable. Interestingly, and not surprisingly, local shops and markets came out best, with 80 per cent of their packaging suitable for recycling.

As consumers, we can help to change this. If enough of us choose goods which have less packaging, or where the packaging can be recycled, the supermarkets will get the message.

Reducing your packaging waste

No-brainer

- Don't add to the packaging problem. Bunches of bananas, melons and pineapples do not need to go into plastic bags – they have their own natural wrappings. So for that matter do cabbages, cauliflowers and lettuces. If supermarket suppliers left the outer leaves on they wouldn't need to shrink wrap them.
- Where there is a choice, buy the ones with least packaging or with recyclable packaging, e.g. fruit juice in glass bottles rather than waxed cardboard or plastic cartons.
- Don't buy individually wrapped portions. A pack of six yogurts, especially the small ones designed for children, has a much lower content to plastic ratio than one large pot – and is much more expensive, ounce for ounce. Buy a big pot and transfer to a small glass jar or reusable plastic pot if small portions are needed for lunch boxes or similar.

Worth doing

- Use your local milkman. You will pay a little more per pint, but the glass bottles can be reused continuously, and having milk – and perhaps other produce – delivered to your door, normally in an electric vehicle, you may be able to reduce your trips (by car) to the shops, and therefore lower your food miles.

- Find out more about how you can help to reduce packaging by visiting the WRAP (Waste & Resources Action Programme) website at **www.wrap.org.uk**.

What sorts of packaging can be recycled?

Much of this is obvious – some less so. And there are some variations, as councils have different systems for dealing with collected materials. You can normally recycle:

- glass, in any form. Currently under one-third of the bottles and jars we buy go into the recycling bins. It should be 100 per cent
- aluminium, again, in any form – cans, food trays, foil, bottle tops. Aluminium takes a lot of energy to extract from the raw ore, but a tiny percentage of this to recover recycled material
- paper and cardboard, but not waxed or lined cardboard drinks containers
- some plastics, e.g. PET (polyethylene terephthalate) used for soft drink bottles is highly recyclable. It can be turned back into new bottles, but is also the raw material for 'polar fleece' a fine wool-substitute. Detergent bottles, milk flagons and similar made from HDPE (high density polyethylene) are also easily recycled, but all too often thrown out – less than 10 per cent are currently recycled. Plastic bags can also be made from HDPE. They are less suitable for recycling because they are harder to identify when materials are being sorted. The thin plastics used for tubs and wrapping is generally not recyclable, mainly because of the sorting problem.

Fairtrade

By historic standards, food is very cheap in the UK. We eat better – and more – for less now than our grandparents did. Falling prices have been partly the result of better productivity, economies of scale and a more efficient distribution system, but they have also dropped because supermarkets have used their huge buying power to drive down the prices they pay farmers. That is a problem for farmers and farm workers in this country, but even more so in developing countries. Too many small farmers and plantation workers growing bananas, pineapples, coffee, tea, sugar cane, avocados and other fruits and tropical products, are not getting a living wage from their work. Too many poor communities are becoming more impoverished as they labour to put cheap food on our supermarket shelves.

The fairtrade movement was started to fight this injustice. It aims to ensure that the growers get a fair share of the profit from their produce, and that their communities begin to lift themselves out of poverty. Fairtrade products are not necessarily more expensive than unfairly traded ones – the difference is that more of the profits go to the growers, and less to the middlemen and retailers.

The Fairtrade Foundation is the main campaigning and certifying body for fairtrade. Any produce which carries its symbol has to meet very clear standards. In a fairtrade deal, farmers are guaranteed a price above the normal market price for their crop which is set for several years, so that they can plan for the long term. No matter how the world market price drops, the farmers will never be paid below the agreed minimum price, but if it rises, they will get a premium above the going rate. The buyer is also required to invest in the local community, helping to pay for schools or health care.

Notice that 'fairtrade' applies to the product not the manufacturer or shipper. You will find fairtrade symbols on products from multinationals such as Nestlé, and you might wonder about the depth of their commitment to the fairtrade cause.

You may prefer to buy fairtrade goods from companies which only deal in these – for example, Cafedirect or the Day Chocolate company (Divine chocolate).

The fairtrade concept began around 20 years ago and is now very well established. At the time of writing, an estimated 5 million farmers in 58 countries benefit from fairtrade deals, and the fairtrade symbol is now carried by over 1,000 foods and drinks, and by some non-food products. Sales have increased dramatically, from around £17 million a year in 1998 – mainly of coffee, the first fairtrade product – to nearly £200 million a year by 2005, and when the latest figures are available they are expected to show continuing dramatic rises.

Fairtrade goods include:

- fresh fruit: apples, avocados, bananas, coconuts, grapes, mangoes, oranges, pears and pineapples
- beverages: cocoa, coffee, tea, beers and wines
- herbs and spices
- honey
- sugar, confectionery and chocolate
- rice and quinoa
- cotton goods, sports balls and flowers.

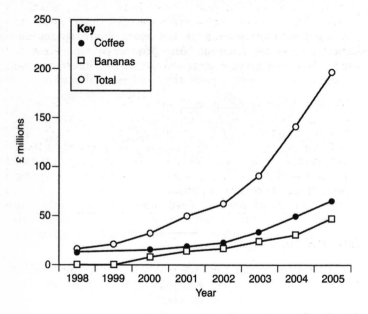

figure 5.10 Fairtrade sales in the UK, 1998 to 2005.

The banana rip-off

In 2007, The Guardian commissioned an analysis of the profits of the big fruit firms – *Dole*, *Chiquita*, *Del Monte* and *Fyffes* – who between them control over 75 per cent of the global market in bananas. This showed how little of the profit went to the grower. When you spend £1 on bananas in the supermarket, 40p goes to the store, 48p goes to the supplier and 12p is taken by the production costs, and of this labour costs form only 1.5p. But it's not just the workers on the plantations and in the packaging plants that are getting ripped off. The fruit firms all work through networks of companies, mainly based in tax havens, and they arrange their costs so that the profits are concentrated where the tax rates are lowest or non-existent. These firms typically pay little tax in the countries where the fruit is grown, little where it is sold, and little in their home country – in fact, they pay very little tax anywhere.

You do not have to contribute to their profits. Fairtrade bananas give a good price to the farm workers, and are shipped by more ethical businesses. Of the supermarkets, Sainsbury's and Waitrose sell only fairtrade bananas, and the Co-op sells fairtrade bananas in all of its stores. The others have not yet got onboard at the time of writing, but consumer choices and campaigning pressure will win through eventually.

No-brainer

If there are equivalent fairtrade and non-fairtrade products on the shelf, buy fairtrade.

Worth doing

- If your supermarket (or greengrocer) does not sell fairtrade goods, ask why not – then go elsewhere to buy them.
- Find out more about the work of the Fairtrade Foundation, and how you can help to spread the fairtrade message. Visit them at **www.fairtrade.org.uk**.

Bottled water

Bottled water represents one of marketing's greatest triumphs over common sense. In the developed world, where most of it is drunk, tap water is better regulated, less likely to contain contaminants, and often tastes better than bottled water – if your tastebuds are sensitive enough to notice the difference (London's tap water regularly outscores bottled varieties in blind tests). In the developing world, where public tap water may be of more varying quality and purity, the availability of bottled water (for those that can afford it) reduces the pressure on governments to make sure that a safe water supply is there for everyone.

Bottled water is bad for the environment. It is estimated that in manufacturing and transporting the plastic bottle, extracting and processing the water and transporting the filled bottle, around 1 litre of oil is used for every 4 litres of water. And 5 litres of water – 6 litres if it is imported – is used to manufacture and transport each litre of bottled water. Further to this, around 90 per cent of the empty bottles are thrown out with the general rubbish, to finish up in landfill.

We move lorry loads of water around the country, taking Highland water to Devon, and Devon water to the Highlands. We import lots of it from France, and from further afield – you can buy water from Hawaii, Japan, India, Canada, even Australia and New Zealand! We currently drink over 2 billion litres of bottled water a year in the UK – and we are relatively light consumers by international standards. In the UK we drink a little under 40 litres per person. In most of Europe, they drink two or three times as much, with Italy topping the list at over 180 litres per person per year (and Italian tap water is safe to drink!).

Bottled water is expensive. Even the own brands cost about 500 times as much as tap water, and people can pay way more for speciality brands. You want to save the environment, and save money?

No-brainer

Don't buy bottled water. If you need a bottle of water when you go out, fill your own bottle from your own tap. If you want cold bottled water when you are out, fill a bottle from the tap the day before and keep it in the fridge.

Summary

- All food production takes energy. With industrialized farming, the food energy you get out is not much more than the fossil fuel energy that goes in – and meat requires much more input energy that it produces.
- We need to reduce our 'food miles' – how far food travels to reach us. We can do this by buying more local foods, and more seasonal foods (which should also be local). We should not be buying any foods which are flown in.
- We should only buy fish from sustainable stocks or that which has been sustainably farmed.
- Factory farming is not ethically acceptable. Buy only free-range poultry and meat.

- Organic farming is environmentally friendly. Organic foods, especially if fresh (and local) taste better.
- A vegan diet is better for the environment. A vegetarian diet has more impact than vegan, but much less than one high in meat.
- We waste far too much food. We need to avoid buying what will not be eaten, and plan our cooking to avoid unwanted surpluses.
- Vegetable peeling and waste can be composted, along with all forms of garden trimmings and green rubbish.
- Unnecessary food packaging is a waste of energy and creates disposal problems. As far as possible, buy foods with minimal packaging, or in reusable containers.
- Fairtrade gives a better deal to the farmers in developing countries. Look for the logo, and support the movement.
- Bottled water is hard to justify.

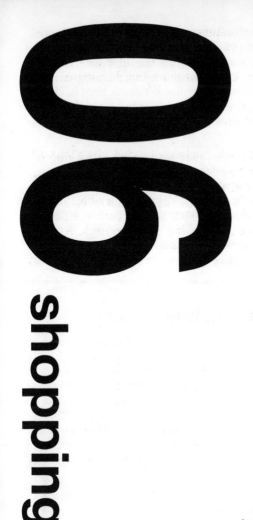

06

shopping

In this chapter you will learn:
- how cheap clothes exploit workers in the Third World
- about environmentally friendly materials
- how energy-saving devices can waste energy
- about fairtrade goods and clothes
- about online ethical shopping.

This is something of a catch-all chapter, to cover things which are not covered elsewhere, but there are common themes. The main one, of course, is that we need to follow the three Rs – reduce, reuse, recycle. We met this earlier when looking at furniture, but it applies equally or more here. If you don't really need it, don't buy it. If you do really need one, would second-hand do? And when you no longer need it, put it back into circulation for reuse, or make sure that its components get recycled.

The next two themes are ones that we met when looking at food, but may be even more relevant here. Many of the clothes, soft furnishings, toys, gadgets and similar small items on sale in our shops are imported. They are racking up a lot of fuel miles between them – mainly by sea, which is more carbon efficient than either land or air transport, but still uses fuel. A high proportion of these imports come from developing countries, where all too often working conditions are appalling and rates of pay are cripplingly low.

Buy less – or even, buy nothing

Our basic problem is that we buy too much. We buy too many clothes, gadgets, toys, books (did you buy this copy, or – environmentally better – borrow it from a friend or the library?) and everything else. If we all bought less, it would reduce the strain on the environment and we might even be the happier for it. (Total credit card debt in the UK is currently estimated to be over £200 billion – and that does not include mortgages, which total over £1 trillion. In the USA, total personal debt – again not counting mortgages – is close to $2 trillion. If we spent less and had less debt hanging over us, wouldn't we be happier?)

Look out for this year's Buy Nothing Day – you can get details from the website at **www.buynothingday.co.uk** – and take the spirit of the movement to heart and try to restrict your purchases all year round. How many coats, pairs of shoes, jumpers do you need? (I suspect that men will find these questions easier to answer than women.) Do you really need to replace your solar-powered mobile phone charger with a new one that's 10 per cent more efficient? (And women will find it easier to say 'No' to that.)

Clothes

There are two key questions we need to ask about clothes: How were they manufactured? What materials are they made from?

Fair wages

In the last two decades, the supermarket approach to retailing – pile them high and sell them cheap – has extended across into clothes. (And, of course, the supermarkets are now clothes retailers –*Tesco*, *Asda*/*Wal-Mart* and *Sainsbury's* are the UK's biggest, in terms of volume.) For the (European or American) customer, this has meant much cheaper clothes; for the manufacturers it is a different story. In Sri Lanka, for example, prices paid to clothes factories have dropped 30 per cent in the last ten years, but those factories have faced a 20 per cent increase in costs for raw materials and energy. There are two ways in which manufacturers can produce more for less: improve the efficiency of the factory by installing new machines and/or adopting better work practices; make the workers do more, for less. (The minimum wage for garment workers in Bangladesh has been £7 per month since 1994. After a strike this year (2007), it was agreed to raise that to £12 per month – and even that is only half a living wage.) The second approach is taken all too often, and we – the shoppers in the West – are part of this exploitation. If price is a major factor in where we buy clothes, retailers will compete to sell at lower prices, and they will get their price cuts by paying their suppliers less. Why can't the suppliers hold out for better prices? Unfortunately, it's all about buying power and global competition. The big chain stores and supermarkets buy in huge quantities, but only on limited contracts, and are willing and able to switch to alternative suppliers at the drop of a T-shirt. And with a few, rare exceptions, the big boys all play the same game.

Labour Behind the Label has been campaigning on behalf of garment workers for some years, with some – albeit limited – progress. But the more people who take up the cause, the more progress they will make, and this is one area where consumer power really can be effective. Find out more about their campaigns, and how you can help by visiting them at **www.labourbehindthelabour.org**.

And if you want to know more about the harsh realities of the clothes industry, read Naomi Klein's *No Logo*.

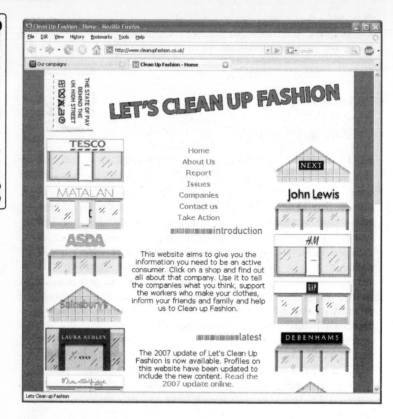

figure 6.1 Let's Clean Up Fashion works in partnership with Labour Behind the Label. It aims to give people the information they need to be able to buy ethically. Visit them at **www.cleanupfashion.co.uk/** and check their ratings of retailers – before you go clothes shopping.

Materials

The basic assumption that natural must be best isn't necessarily true. **Cotton** is a prime example. It is one of the most water-intensive and environmentally damaging products – and the pollution starts in the fields and continues in the factories. Developing countries use around 300,000 tonnes of pesticides each year, and half of this goes on cotton alone – and that works out at half a cupful for every T-shirt! This is destroying eco-systems and killing people. The Pesticide Action Network (PAN) estimate that over 20,000 people a year die from pesticide poisoning in the Third World. (To find out more about this problem, visit PAN at **www.pan-uk.org.**)

Growing and processing both require huge quantities of water – in total about 1,000 litres per T-shirt. The inputs for this may be diverting water from better uses elsewhere, or lowering river levels or the water table – competition for water is already a problem in many parts of Africa, the Middle East and Asia, and the scale and scope of the problem is increasing. The outputs carry pesticides and fertilizers off the land, and cleansing and dyeing chemicals from the factories.

Organic cotton – grown without pesticides or synthetic fertilizers – is a big step forward, but not the end of the road. It really needs to be fairtrade grown, unbleached and/or naturally dyed. The dyes are probably the biggest sticking point. Natural, vegetable dyes tend to have a limited colour range, but what's more of a problem is that the colourant is such a small part of the plant that you need to grow a lot to get a little dye, which makes it very expensive. According to the Journal of the Society of Dyers and Colourists, to dye 1 kg of cotton will cost 20p with synthetics and over £40 with natural dyes. They also estimate that to switch all wool and cotton dyeing to natural products, you would need to devote nearly one third of the world's farmland to growing dye crops.

Hemp is a very versatile crop, though one that has fallen out of use – largely because of restrictions on its cultivation, especially in the US and UK. These are now being lifted, as the powers that be have at last recognized that textile hemp and marijuana hemp are two different plants. Hemp fibres are tough enough to be made into rope, but can be soft and fine enough to be made into lace; used by itself or combined with cotton, silk or other textiles, it can be spun into yarn for knitting or woven into fabrics. The plant's seeds are a good source of proteins and oils; the woody core can be used for paper-making; and anything left over can be burnt as biomass fuel or converted to bio-diesel or ethanol. Altogether a very useful plant, and one that can be grown without damaging the environment.

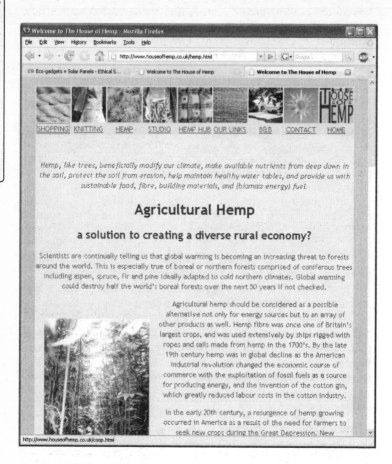

figure 6.2 Find out more about hemp, and buy hemp clothes, fabrics and yarns at the House of Hemp (**www.houseofhemp.co.uk**). You will also find an interesting range of hemp garments at *The Hemp Trading Company* (**http://www.thtc.co.uk**).

Bamboo is textile that people are just beginning to appreciate. It has all the advantages of cotton, and more, and does not have cotton's environmental costs. Bamboo fibres are hollow and much thinner than cotton fibres, producing fabrics that are very soft, and breathable, wicking moisture away from the skin. They are also antibacterial, antifungal and offer a high level of UV protection. Bamboo is a fully renewable resource. The plant is grown without artificial fertilizers – and on land that is too poor for other crops. The range of bamboo clothing currently on the market is limited, but well worth investigating. In the UK at present, Bamboo Clothes (**www.bambooclothes.com**) probably has the best range; other suppliers include Bam (**www.bambooclothing.co.uk**) and Bamboo Wear (**www.bamboo-wear.co.uk**).

Linen is the most ancient of all fabrics, going back at least 5,000 years. It had been very largely replaced by synthetic fibres, but is now starting to make a comeback. It is produced from flax, which grows faster than cotton and requires considerably less fertilizers or pesticides. The production process also requires fewer chemicals. Linen is stronger than cotton, but less flexible so garments wrinkle more easily and are more likely to fray along collars and cuffs. It is excellent for cool summer clothes.

Polyester fleece may not be natural, but it is eco-friendly – its main ingredient is the PET plastic from recycled soft drinks bottles (with about 5 per cent new polyester). The fabric is warm, washable, breathable and much used for blankets, sportswear, sweaters and similar.

Unwanted clothing

Old clothes are a valuable resource. If there's life left in a garment, there's probably someone, somewhere, who would be happy to wear it. Clothes may become unwanted after very little wear – children grow out of things, and adults change shape (intentionally or otherwise); garments may be bought for specific occasions, and have no purpose afterwards. The charity shops do a sterling job of recycling clothing, with very little going to waste. Garments which are likely to sell in their shops go onto the rails, others which are wearable but no longer sellable are collected for shipment out to Third World countries. And those which are really beyond wear are sent on to reclamation companies who can find a use for most types of fabrics. Woolen garments can be reduced to fibres for reworking into new yarn; cotton and silk are made into wiping rags for industry, or used in paper-making; some are chopped to make felt for insulating and lining – there's very little wasted.

If you would like to get something back for your clothes, then look out for clothes exchange shops – there are a few around, generally specializing in certain types of clothes. Online, you'll find What's Mine is Yours, which handles vintage and designer clothing (**http://www.whatsmineisyours.com/**); and the Maternity Exchange (**www.maternityexchange.co.uk**) which buys and sells – and hires for special occasions – maternity clothes.

Ethical fashion?

Can fashion be ethical? Cheap copies of designer garments, made in Third World sweatshops clearly cannot be ethical. Anything which incorporates fur or leather is going to raise problems for some people, and there are environmental issues with the way some crops are grown. But even with garments made from fairly traded renewable materials, for fair wages in good working conditions, there is still a problem. What is in fashion today will be out of fashion next season (though it might come back in again in 20 years). Inevitably, the fashionable dresser's clothes will go out of use long before they are worn out, and then what happens? If they are simply thrown away, that's a waste of resources; if they are hung up or packed away and never actually worn again, that is just as much of a waste; if they are swapped or sold on or donated to a charity shop, then that will extend their life and make better use of the materials and energy that went into their production – it's a shame that it doesn't happen very often.

Style is a different matter. Style can be ethical. Stylish clothes, well-made (by properly paid workers, of course) from good quality (renewable, eco-friendly) material, look good, feel good and last longer.

figure 6.3 Style Will Save Us is a digital fashion magazine with an eco message. They only cover clothes that are fairtrade and/or made from organic or other sustainable materials. They are also strong on recycling, with links to vintage clothing boutiques and swap shops. Visit them at **www.stylewillsaveus.com**.

How can I dress greener?

No-brainer

- **Don't buy cheap clothes** made in Third World sweatshops. Visit Let's Clean Up Fashion (**www.cleanupfashion.co.uk/**) before you start shopping, and support those stores that are trying hardest to ensure that their garments are produced ethically.

- **Don't throw away clothes** when they are no longer wanted. If they are wearable, donate them to a charity shop or swap or sell them through a clothes exchange. If they are really worn out, those made from absorbent fabrics can be cut up into rags and used in place of paper kitchen towels – it's more eco-friendly to wash and dry rags than to throw away single-use paper towels. And when all else fails, look for a textiles recycling point.

Worth doing

- **Buy organic** – It's the environmentally friendly thing to do, and generally speaking, garments made from organic cotton, wool, bamboo, hemp or whatever will have been fairly traded and fairly made – though this is more likely to be true with smaller retailers than with the big boys. You can find a comprehensive list of retailers at About Organics (**www.aboutorganics.co.uk**) – look for the Organic Clothing link.

- **Buy second-hand** – You would be surprised at what turns up. And sales of clothing are an important source of income for many charities.

- **Buy to last** – Choose garments that will wear well, and that you will want to wear for a long time.

- **Buy recycled** – Or rather, buy clothes with some recycled content, if possible. At the moment there is no standard labelling system to indicate this, so you cannot always tell.

Gadgets

There are lots of gadgets on offer for the environmentally aware – solar-powered battery chargers, wind-up radios, water-powered batteries, smart sockets that turn themselves off when an appliance goes on standby, foot-powered electricity generators.

Must-do

Three questions to ask before buying any of these:

1 Will you actually use it? Because if an energy-saving device is not used, then the energy that went into its manufacture has been wasted. A wind-up radio is a great idea, but only for someone who likes to listen to the radio outdoors or on the move and doesn't already have a portable radio – it's almost certainly eco-friendlier to recharge batteries than to manufacture a new device.

2 Does it serve a useful purpose? There are multi-sockets that will cut power to all a computer's peripherals when the computer itself is turned off, and remote control devices that will turn off the mains power, instead of leaving appliances on standby. Very clever, but doesn't a finger on a switch do the same job?

3 If you are buying gadgets as gifts, will the recipients use them, and are they likely to already have them?

The crucial point is that much of our current trouble stems from over-consumption. The way out has to be by buying less, not buying more – gadgets, in particular, should be looked at with a very critical eye.

H_2O battery

A water-powered battery? This is worth investigating! The power comes from an electro-chemical reaction between its electrodes, which takes place when there is water present to carry the electric current (so the batteries can be stored, dry, for years without deteriorating). To activate it, simply fill with water – and top it up from time to time as it evaporates. After two years of continuous use the reaction between the electrodes dwindles and the battery needs replacing – but all its components are recyclable. So, whether it's actually 'powered' by water or not, here we have a non-polluting, recyclable battery, suitable for low-demand devices such as clocks and calculators. You can find these at most eco-stores – but before buying one, remember to apply the gadget rules!

figure 6.4 The Ethical Superstore has lots of eco-gadgets – in fact it probably has the widest range of environmentally friendly, energy-saving, organic and/or fairtrade goods of all types to be found in any online store. Visit it at **www.ethicalsuperstore.com**.

Gifts

Being ethical does not have to mean being joyless. The art of giving is an important part of social bonding – and receiving gifts is a pleasure. Let's try and give ethically.

- **Buy fairtrade.** Buying goods from Third World producers at fair prices helps them to build their future – and you get a quality product. We've already met fairtrade food and drink, but you can also buy clothes, sheets and towels, candles, paper goods, toys, ornaments and other craft goods through fairtrade retailers.

figure 6.5 Traidcraft is the UK's leading fairtrade organization, dedicated to getting a better deal for farmers and craftspeople in developing countries. To find out more about them, or to go fairtrade shopping, see **www.traidcraftshop.co.uk**.

- **Give a donation.** Several charities run donations-as-gifts schemes, where you pay for a specific item, e.g. a goat, some packets of seeds, a school desk or support for a project, to be given in the recipient's name. You will then have a card to give to the other person telling them about the donation. What your recipient gets out of it is a nice warm feeling. Traidcraft (**www.traidcraftshop.co.uk**) offer a limited number of 'Gifts for life'; Oxfam (**www.oxfam.org.uk**) has a much wider range of donations in their 'Unwrapped' selection.
- **Give a loan.** This is similar to giving a donation, except that here you can make an interest-free loan to a specific person in a developing country, to help them to expand or to get a business off the ground. As the loans are almost always repaid in full and on time, all that you lose is the interest. Find out more at **www.kiva.org**.

figure 6.6 Give a gift of giving through Oxfam Unwrapped – or set up your own wedding list or wish list so that people can give to you. Head for **www.oxfam.org.uk** and look for the Unwrapped link.

Flowers – the perfect gift?

What gift could be more natural – or ethical – than a bouquet of flowers? Well, actually, lots of things! The problem is that a lot of the flowers sold in the UK are flown in from abroad. We currently import almost 20 tonnes of flowers a year from Kenya, and that generates an awful lot of CO_2. Colombia is another major exporter to the UK – and that's even more air miles for every bloom. The flower retailers reply that the alternative is to grow them here with artificial light and heat, which have their own environmental costs. You could take the same approach as with food and buy only local, seasonal flowers, and if the choice gets rather limited over the winter, there are also late berries and early bulbs, and indoor plants. However, there is now a middle way. The Fair Flowers Fair Plants initiative is encouraging low-impact sustainable cultivation. It is still in its early stage, so you will not find participating retailers everywhere yet. Look for their logo when you next buy flowers.

fair flowers
fair plants

Plastic shopping bags

While we are on the subject of shopping, let's pause for a few moments to think about shopping bags. We get through a staggering number of plastic shopping bags every year – estimates range from 12 to 18 billion plastic bags just from the supermarkets (small shops and local markets also give them to their customers). That's upwards of 200 bags per person per year! Why do we use so many? And where do they all go?

We use them because they are there and they are 'free' and we are too lazy to think ahead and take bags with us when we go shopping. (Note the quotation marks – they are not free, it's just that the cost is hidden in the other things that you buy. UK retailers spend around £70 million a year on plastic bags.)

Most plastic bags currently finish up in landfill – though some blow around the streets and countryside, or clog the rivers and seas. Scientists estimate that it will take 500 years for the average plastic bag to decay in landfill – it will be the twenty-fifth century before we have accurate figures. The decay rate is faster while they are loose in the environment, but they are a real danger to wildlife. Less than 1 per cent of plastic bags are currently recycled. They all could be.

The campaigns against plastic bags

We don't actually need disposable plastic shopping bags. In fact, there are whole countries that are managing without them.

Free, single-use plastic bags have been banned completely in Bangladesh, Rwanda, Tanzania, South Africa and Taiwan because of the environmental damage they cause – in Bangladesh discarded bags blocking the drainage system was found to have been a major cause of the flooding in 1988 and 1998.

In Denmark and Ireland, taxes on bags have dramatically reduced their use – down 95 per cent in Ireland.

Under voluntary pacts, supermarkets in Hong Kong and France have stopped giving out single-use plastic bags – they have been banned completely in Paris.

The question is, what to use in place of thin, single-use plastic bags? One solution is thick, reusable plastic bags. In many countries, supermarkets are offering these to shoppers, at a nominal cost, as 'bags for life'. When they start to tear – in practice, after 30 to 50 trips, depending upon what you put in them – the supermarkets replace them free of charge. And the old bags are all recycled. They have been in use in the UK for some years now, but only carry a small percentage of the shopping home. Why? Because the supermarkets are still giving away thin ones. If there are no free bags, and the choice is between buying new 'bags for life' or remembering to bring your old ones (or proper shopping bags and baskets) with you – as happens in French supermarkets – people bring bags.

At the time of writing, the UK government and retail industry seem to be slowly edging towards doing something about this. There's a voluntary agreement to reduce bag use by one quarter in the next year – though exactly how they will persuade shoppers to take fewer bags remains unclear. London council is discussing either following the example of Paris and banning them completely, or alternatively levying a 10p per bag tax.

Bag-free towns

Fortunately, there are some people who don't wait for the government to get its act together. In May 2007, Modbury in South Devon became a plastic-bag free town. Its 43 traders, the Co-op, the butcher, fruit shop and vet all agreed to stop giving away plastic bags for a trial period of six months. The experiment was obviously a success, because at the end of that time, they all agreed to make the ban permanent. Shoppers have overwhelmingly supported the initiative, because (a) they appreciate that they are 'doing their bit for the environment' and (b) once you have got used to it, there is no hardship in living without plastic bags.

How have they managed without? Long-lasting woven cotton bags were ordered, for sale to the locals, and have been taken up enthusiastically. And where some form of containers have been needed for goods, they have used bags made of paper or cornstarch (which are impermeable, like plastic bags, but fully bio-degradable), or boxes of recycled cardboard.

At the time of writing, late 2007, another 50 towns have followed Modbury's example.

No-brainer

Buy yourself enough shopping bags – preferably made from natural materials such as cotton or jute, but otherwise long-lasting plastic 'bags for life' – to cope with your shopping habits and remember to take them with you (that's the tricky bit until it becomes ingrained).

Worth doing

Start a campaign to turn your town or local high street into a plastic-bag free zone. You can find out how Modbury did it at their website **www.plasticbagfree.com**.

Ethical retailers and shopping guides

This is just a small selection of online ethical retailers.

Ethical Company Organisation – www.ethical-company-organisation.org

This looks at the companies, not just the goods, matching them to ethical and environmental criteria, and giving comparative information on literally thousands of companies and brands. It publishes the *Good Shopping Guide*, a valuable reference book if you are serious about who you shop and do business with, and also runs the gooshing site:

gooshing – www.gooshing.co.uk

This is a shopping guide, ranking goods mainly on ethical rating of the companies that produce them. There's a simple star rating but, if you want it, there is more detailed information, showing whether the company has a positive or negative record in respect of animal testing, armaments, boycotts, ecological schemes, environmental reporting, genetic modification, nuclear power and political donations. Not everyone would regard all of these in the same way – there are arguments both ways on animal testing and genetic modification, for example – so your personal rating of a company may vary from gooshing's star ranking. Prices are usually but not always given, to help you get best value.

The Green Providers Directory – www.search-for-me.co.uk

A comprehensive directory of firms offering green, organic and fairtrade products and services.

Guide me green – www.guidemegreen.com

A UK-based directory of green companies, covering accommodation, food, travel, magazines and charities as well as retailers.

A lot of organics – http://www.alotoforganics.co.uk

UK organic directory and search engine, covering a full spectrum of organic producers, retailers and other organizations.

Natural Collection – www.naturalcollection.com

This is an eco-friendly department store, selling eco gadgets, recycled products (e.g. glassware, paper), fairtrade and organic clothing, natural cleaning products, etc.

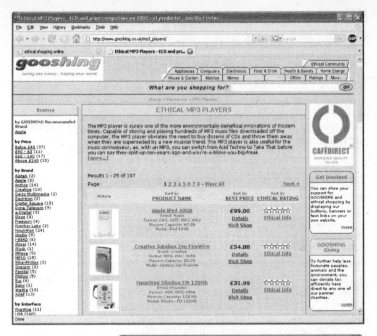

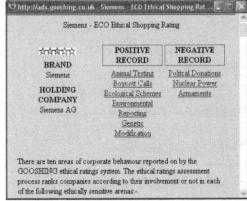

figure 6.7 At gooshing, you can look up a type of product and see the ethical rating of its manufacturers, with detailed ethical info available if wanted.

Get ethical – www.getethical.com

Another well-stocked store – and with a good choice of books and musical instruments, as well as the usual clothes, fashion accessories, ornaments and beauty products.

Greener Living – www.greenerliving.co.uk

Sells only products that are zero or low carbon, and which can help reduce your ecological footprint. They also have articles, tips and advice on greener living.

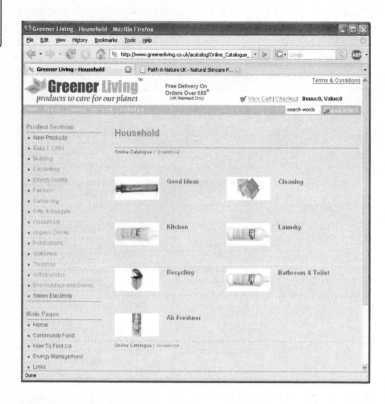

figure 6.8 Greener Living online store has a wide range of products, and is very easy to navigate. Try it at **www.greenerliving.co.uk**.

The Ethical Living Company – www.theethicallivingcompany.com

Sells organic cotton towels, baby clothes, soaps, beauty products and recycled glassware.

People Tree – http://www.peopletree.co.uk

Sells mainly organic and fair trade clothing for men, women and children, with some accessories and homewares.

TerraPlana – http://shop.terraplana.com

Sells shoes and accessories made from vegetable (chrome-free) tanned leather, natural latex, recycled rubber, wood from managed forests and other sustainable, non-polluting materials. Not cheap, but stylish!

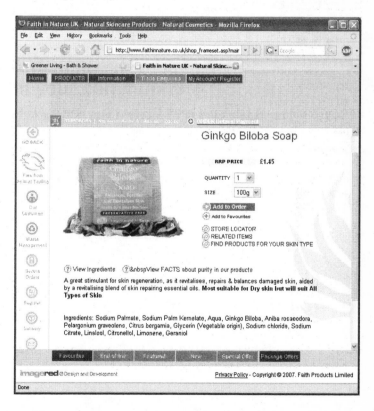

figure 6.9 Like many of the better environmentally conscious suppliers, Faith in Nature clearly lists its products' ingredients on their website. Visit them at **www.faithinnature.co.uk**.

Faith in Nature – www.faithinnature.co.uk

A long-established Scottish firm specializing in natural hair and beauty products.

Ethical Consumer magazine – www.ethicalconsumer.org

The website of the magazine. This is published six times a year, and carries reports about all manner of products and services, rated against their own very strict ethical guidelines. For an annual subscription (currently £20) you can access these reports in their Ethiscore database. The site also organizes its own and supports others' consumer boycotts.

Summary

- Most cheap clothes have been made in the Third World by people working for very low wages in poor conditions.
- Look for fairtrade, ethically-made clothes.
- Organic cotton, bamboo, hemp and linen are renewable resources – and can be made into feel-good, look-good clothes.
- Energy-saving gadgets only save energy if they are regularly used in place of devices which consume energy.
- Unwanted, unused gifts are a simple waste of resources. Aim to buy what will be used, and buy fairtrade when you can.
- The online ethical shopping guides and directories can help you track down suppliers and retailers.

07

money

In this chapter you will learn:
- about ethical banks, and how few of them there are
- about environmental issues and mortgages
- how ethical investing can be better for your money.

Money may or may not be the root of all evil, but it can certainly be put to evil purposes. Our concern should be to ensure that our money is used to support only environmentally-friendly, people-friendly, peaceful, fair purposes. Because our money is actively used, whether we are aware of it or not. The money held in our accounts – current or savings, and the money we pay into our private/company pension fund is being loaned or invested by the banks and pension funds in all manner of ways. We can take control of this, and make sure that our money is only used for ethical purposes.

Banking

This is an area where the choice is very, very simple. There is only one UK bank that operates and invests according to strict ethical conditions, and offers the full range of banking services to personal customers. That bank is the Co-operative. This is part of the wider Co-operative Wholesale Society, and its members have always been strong on issues of peace, justice and fair dealing. In 1991 the bank found that the majority of its customers would welcome a clear ethical policy on investments. One was introduced, initially banning loans to any companies involved in the arms trade or human rights violations in any form, and supporting organizations with socially useful purposes. It has continued to consult its customers regularly, to ensure that its ethical policy reflects their concerns.

The Co-operative Bank will not invest in any business involved in:

- the manufacture or sale of arms or torture equipment, or with links to any government that violates human rights
- socially irresponsible activities, including tobacco manufacture and sale, currency speculation, and genetic modification
- environmental damage, through fossil fuel production, the manufacture of dangerous chemicals, unsustainable use of natural resources, e.g. timber or fish
- mistreatment of animals through testing, intensive farming, blood sports or the fur trade.

It supports:

- businesses who promote fairtrade and labour rights for their workers and those of their suppliers
- charities, co-operatives and credit unions
- businesses involved in recycling, renewable energy and sustainable development
- organic and free-range farming.

The Bank is also working hard to reduce its own environmental impact, and publishes an annual Sustainability Report setting out its economic, social and ecological targets, and how much progress it has made over the year.

figure 7.1 Visit the Co-operative Bank online at **www.co-operativebank.co.uk** and find out more about their ethical policy.

If you want a current account with a truly ethical bank, the choice is then very simple: do you choose a branch-based account with the Co-operative Bank, or an online account with Smile, the Co-operative Movement's internet bank. Internet banking is not convenient if you need to pay in cheques or cash regularly, but it does offer better interest rates on its savings and current account.

figure 7.2 Ethical money, but with better interest rates, at Smile (**www.smile.co.uk**).

The other ethical banks

There are two other ethical banks operating in the UK, but neither provides the full banking service to personal customers.

Tridos, a Netherlands-based company, offers only savings accounts to individuals, as its focus is ethical businesses. For these it provides the full range of current accounts, savings and loans (Tridos is Cafedirect's banker, and rightly proud of it). It also has a venture capital arm that specializes in finance for solar and wind energy projects, organic farming and similar developments. Find out more about Tridos on the web at **www.triodos.co.uk**.

The **Charity Bank** is a registered charity which is also a bank. Its purpose is to provide low interest loans for charitable activities, and it takes deposits from people who are happy to know that their money is doing good, even though it may be earning less interest than it could have earned elsewhere. The bank normally pays up to 2 per cent interest, though it did initially take deposits into its CITRA (community investment tax relief) fund which, with tax relief actually worth 7 per cent a year, was better than ordinary bank accounts.

Find out more about their work and how you can put your money to work ethically, at **www.charitybank.org**.

In the USA, Wainwright Bank & Trust Company works to very similar ethical principles, as does Grupo Financiero FINSOL in Mexico, GLS bank in Germany and Banca Popolare Etica, in Italy and Spain.

Islamic banking

Islamic banking is based on the values behind Shariah law, which aims to protect the five 'pillars' of an Islamic society – faith, life, wealth, intellect and posterity. Shariah law bans paying or receiving interest, but permits the payment of dividends on shares. An Islamic bank will not invest in any company which is involved in alcohol, tobacco, gambling, armaments, pornography, pork or finance (which could be charging interest or investing in unacceptable activities).

You do not have to be a Muslim to use an Islamic bank. For more information contact the Institute of Islamic Banking and Insurance at **www.islamic-banking.com**.

Mortgages

Apart from the Co-operative Bank, the most ethical source of mortgages at present must be the **Ecology Building Society**. This was set up just over 25 years ago to promote sustainable housing and provides mortgages only for ecologically beneficial, energy-efficient housing or renovation projects. They carry their commitment to sustainability through into their own offices and practices, and their care for people is shown in their attitude to borrowers. They will not lend more than three times earnings, because they do not want people to be over-stretched.

If you are looking for a mortgage for a new build, a conversion or for buying woodlands or even a houseboat mooring, then find out more about them at **www.ecology.co.uk**.

Among the mainstream companies, the Norwich & Peterborough Building Society offer 'Green' and 'Brown' mortgages. Green mortgages are for new, energy-efficient houses – those with a SAP (Standard Assessment Procedure) rating of 100 or higher – and for energy improvements to existing properties. To add some extra 'greenery' to this, they plant 40 trees for every mortgage they issue. The Brown mortgages are for converting or restoring property, and the environmentally-friendly aspect to this is that it is better to build on a 'brownfield' site than on farmland/open space. Have a closer look at **www.npbs.co.uk**.

Several other building societies are currently also offering to plant trees when you take out mortgages with them. Look out for the offers – but assess their real value and costs as carefully as you would any others.

Ethical investment

With any form of savings, whether it is your child's trust fund, your ISA or your pension, security is important. You need to know that the money will be there when you need it, and that it will have grown nicely in the meantime. Fortunately, security and ethics are not incompatible. Friends Provident set up the first ethical investment fund in 1984, and it showed that ethical does not have to mean unprofitable – on the contrary, ethical funds have consistently done as well as, and sometimes better than, funds where the only criteria is the search for profits. In 2007, for example, the Co-operative Insurance Sustainable (CIS) Leaders trust, was the top performing trust in the UK, with growth of nearly 30 per cent, compared to the industry average of 13 per cent.

One of the key organizations in this field is EIRIS, Ethical Investment Research Services, which was set up in 1983 by a group of charities and churches who wanted to ensure that their own investments met ethical criteria. EIRIS has been assessing companies ever since, but also works with those companies and with investment fund managers to promote ethical practice and socially responsible investment. You can find out more about their work and get general advice on ethical investment at their website, **www.eiris.org**. What you won't find is any specific advice on which fund to use. For this you need to look elsewhere.

Ethical Investors Group is ethical in more than just name – these people are top of the Guardian's Giving List, donating 50 per cent of their pre-tax profits to charities (compared to the 1–2 per cent that most companies manage). They give advice on pensions, mortgages, ISAs and insurance. Their ethical fund guide lists over 50 leading funds with their ratings, which they divide into three areas:

- Humanist – including human rights, the arms trade, pornography, tobacco, gambling and alcohol
- Animal welfare – covering animal testing, and the food industry
- Environment – a broad area, looking for commitment to environmental protection.

As well as the ratings, there is more detailed information about each fund's policies on ethical issues. To read more, go to the Ethical Investors Group at **www.ethicalinvestors.co.uk** and follow the link to the Ethical Fund Directory.

There are many other financial advisers who are willing to give advice on ethical investment. You will find a directory of them at the Ethical Investment Association **www.ethicalinvestment. org.uk**.

Shareholder action

For most of us, any investments will be in one sort of fund or another, but we can also invest directly in companies – either those whose aims and practices we support, or those that do things that we do not approve of. And why would you invest in an unethical company? Because that way you can go to the annual shareholders' meeting and try to bring them to account. You only need one share to be able to propose a resolution to be put to shareholders (though you can only propose it – whether it is put or not depends on other things) or to speak at the meeting. In the current climate, with the growing realization that ethical behaviour can pay dividends and that unethical activities can store up costs for the longer term, it may not take much of a push to get the ball rolling.

Managing your money ethically

Must-do

- Think hard about moving your current and savings accounts to Smile or the Co-operative Bank.
- If you are about to set up a child's trust fund, an ISA or a pension fund, look for one where your money will be invested in ethical companies.

Worth doing

Buy a share in a company and see if you can influence its policies.

Summary

- There is only one high street bank that operates strict ethical criteria, and that is the Co-operative Bank.
- Smile is an online alternative to the Co-operative Bank.
- The Ecology Building Society is the only one dedicated to energy-efficient housing, though some others do offer incentives for lowing environmental impact.
- Ethical investment funds can perform as well as ordinary funds.

08

motoring

In this chapter you will learn:
- how much transport contributes to climate change
- how to maximize your car's efficiency
- about the total lifetime energy costs of cars
- about alternatives to fossil fuels
- how electric cars can be good for your pocket and the environment
- how to choose a new car.

Cars are a blessing and a curse. They have given us the freedom to travel where we will, but at huge environmental costs – global warming, air pollution, noise nuisance, the destruction of the landscape with ribbons of tarmac are just the worst of these costs.

CO_2 emissions are probably the single most urgent of these problems. Road transport is currently responsible for almost a quarter of the total CO_2 emissions in the UK, and around 15 per cent of the total worldwide. These figures have increased dramatically in the last 25 years, and are expected to continue to increase for some time. In 1980, the 12 million or so cars and taxis on Britain's roads travelled 140 billion miles a year; by 2000, 24 million vehicles were travelling 240 billion miles a year; by 2010 there are likely to be nearly 35 million cars and taxis in the UK, clocking up over 300 billion miles between them. That's just in the UK, and it doesn't include trucks and lorries. Globally, the total number of motor vehicles is expected to top 1 billion by 2025, and they will be discharging nearly 2,000 million tonnes of CO_2 into the atmosphere.

Petrol and CO_2

A litre of petrol produces 2.8 kilograms of CO_2. A small, fuel-efficient family car will run at an average of around 45 mpg, or 10 miles per litre. That's 0.28 kg of CO_2 per mile. Put it another way. If the supermarket is 2 miles away and you nip down in the car for a pint of milk, you will produce more than 1 kg of CO_2.

Air pollution is the second most pressing problem. Vehicles are responsible for a very large part of most pollutant emissions, especially in cities. In London, 99 per cent of carbon monoxide, 90 per cent of hydrocarbons and 76 per cent of nitrogen oxides are produced by traffic. Where levels of particulates (fine dust and soot) are high, road traffic is typically responsible for 75–85 per cent of this.

Traffic is bad for your health. Particulate emissions damage lungs and lead to increased risks of asthma and heart attacks – it is said that living in Glasgow, Britain's third most polluted city, is as bad for you as smoking over 40 cigarettes a day. According to the Department of Health, the deaths of between 12,000 and 24,000 people a year are accelerated by air pollution.

Catalytic converters reduce the levels of pollutant emissions, but are not without side effects. They convert nitrogen oxide to harmless oxygen and nitrogen, carbon monoxide to carbon dioxide, and unburnt hydrocarbons to carbon dioxide and water. As a result, the exhausts are less harmful, but the car now produces more CO_2. The converters also reduce the overall efficiency of the engine – again producing more CO_2.

If we really want to reduce the environmental impact of cars, then the answer is simple: until that time when there are electric- or hydrogen-powered cars, charged and fuelled from renewable sources, we need to use smaller, more efficient cars, to drive them more economically and to use them less.

Do you really need your car?

The first and most essential question you need to ask yourself is: 'Do I really need a car?' Will public transport, walking, cycling, perhaps with the occasional taxi and car hire, do the job? In the UK, the reality of public transport is that you are probably only going to be able to answer 'yes' to this second question if you live in London or another big city. The further you get into the countryside, the more difficult life becomes without a car. But do think about it – and do the sums. If you do not use your car much, the ongoing costs of maintenance, tax, insurance and depreciation add significantly to the average cost per mile. It can get to a point where it is cheaper to dispose of the car and hire a taxi for those journeys where public transport and muscle power won't do.

What does your car cost you?

Take a few minutes to find out the real cost of your motoring. Work through the simplified calculations below, or use the rather more refined car cost calculator at the Environmental Transport Association.

Capital cost				Example	Your car
	A	Cost to buy		£16,000	
	B	Expected value when you sell		£ 6,000	
	C	Capital cost (A – B)		£10,000	
	D	No of years owned		5	
Annual costs	E	Annual depreciation (C/D)		£2,000	
	F	Tax		£115	
	G	Insurance		£385	
	H	Maintenance, average		£500	
	I	Total annual costs		£3,000	
	J	Annual mileage		5,000	
Mileage costs		Capital costs per mile		60p	
	K	Average mpg		36	
	L	Miles per litre (K/4.5)		8	
	M	Cost per litre		£1	
	N	Fuel cost per mile		12p	
	O	Total cost per mile		72p	
	P	Total annual cost (O x J)		£3,600	

This example was based on a family car which is not used that much. If the same car was used for a regular commute, say 10,000 miles a year, the total annual cost would rise to £4,200, though the cost per mile would go down to 42p. Notice the capital costs per mile figure. If you live in a city and mainly use public transport or walk to get around – so that your annual mileage is very low – this can get alarmingly high.

Two figures to bear in mind when looking at your mileage costs and annual costs:

- taxis currently cost about £2.40 a mile
- you can hire a car from £20 a day.

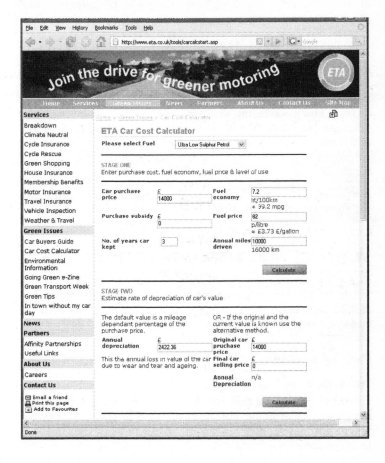

figure 8.1 The car cost calculator at the ETA site. Do your sums at
http://www.eta.co.uk/tools/carcalcstart.asp.

Fuel consumption and pollution are not the only issues. As well as having to be refuelled constantly, a car must first be manufactured, from raw and processed materials, then transported to its point of sale, repaired and maintained throughout its life, and disposed of at the end. You need to look at use of resources and energy over the whole of its lifespan and the environmental impact of disposal.

In practice, ethics are rarely the only consideration in how we choose and use a car. We all have to travel to a greater or lesser extent. What varies are the distance, the number of people that are travelling together, the quantity of equipment to be carried with the people, the feasibility of public transport, and other factors. These determine whether or not a car must be used, and what size and type of car. (For some people, the choice of size and style of car has little to do with practical or ethical considerations, and is much more a matter of perceived status. I would hope that the ethical consumer can rise above this.)

But before we tackle 'Which car?' let's see how you can lower the environmental and energy cost of an existing car.

Working with what you've got

If you have to have a car, the least you can do is to try to maximize your miles per gallon (mpg) and minimize your CO_2 and noxious emissions – fuel-efficient driving is the 'no-brainer' and the 'must-do' here.

Before you start

Travel light

Don't carry anything that you don't need on that journey. If the baby's staying at home, you don't need the buggy in the boot; if you're not playing golf again until next Thursday, the clubs can be unloaded into the house. Every extra pound lowers your mpg.

Rack off

Roof racks and boxes create turbulence over the car, increasing drag and wind resistance. Even an unloaded rack will increase fuel consumption by 2 to 3 per cent. If your car normally does 40 mpg, with the roof rack on you will burn an extra gallon of petrol every 1,000 miles.

Pump up

Under-inflated tyres increase fuel consumption – 1 per cent extra for every 6 psi under the proper pressure – and they wear out faster, so that's a double cost to you and the environment. Worn tyres also affect fuel efficiency, as well as being dangerous. When you are buying new tyres, choose those which give better fuel performance. Radial tyres will normally give better fuel economy than non-radial – typically 4 per cent better – because they distort less in contact with the road and so have lower resistance. Some tyres are sold as 'eco-friendly', because of their performance improvements, for example Michelin's low rolling resistance range. These are claimed to give 2.5 per cent better fuel efficiency than standard radial tyres.

Keep it in good condition

Regular maintenance and servicing is crucial. A dirty air filter will reduce air intake and lead to incomplete combustion, wasting fuel. Worn or incorrectly set spark plugs will also send unburned petrol out through the exhaust. The oil is there to reduce friction in the engine – as it gets older and dirtier, it does not lubricate so well. Have it changed regularly, and use good quality multi-grade oil.

Plan the trip

Decide if it is really necessary. Do you have to pop down to the shops/library/post office/Aunty Edna's today? Could you wait for another day or two and combine it with other errands? Do you need to see that client/supplier/consultant face-to-face, or could it be done over the phone or internet? (You can run video phones across the web nowadays, and swap documents at the same time – virtual meetings can be every bit as productive as roomed ones.)

Is the car the best way to get there? Actually, we already know that it's not the best way, in environmental terms, but is it actually the most convenient and/or economical way to get there? How long will it take compared to public transport? And how does the cost of petrol compare to the fare? What will parking cost – and can you be sure of finding anywhere to park?

If you must go, pick your time and your route to get the smoothest run. A steady 60 or 65 mph on a good road or motorway gives you better mpg than accelerating and braking up and down on country roads or struggling through congestion in towns. If you are stuck in a traffic jam, your engine is running at 0 mpg, and it doesn't get any worse than that.

Can you share the journey with anyone else? If you are commuting or doing the school run, aren't there other people in your area making the same trip?

On the road

Go with the flow

Relax, don't get stressed, enjoy the ride, and take your time. Just about all of the techniques for good, safe, fuel-efficient driving flow from this. Aggressive driving uses more fuel, puts more wear on the tyres, brakes, suspension and engine, and makes other road-users more inclined to drive badly in response to the situations you create. Be cool and you'll add less to global warming.

Drive with a light foot

Accelerating gently and braking gently reduces wear on the brakes and engine, and can improve fuel efficiency by up to 30 per cent. It also makes little difference to total travelling time, especially in the stop-start of town traffic. Watch the road well ahead and aim for as smooth a speed as possible. In queues, for example, you should try to maintain a steady speed, even if this allows a gap to open ahead of you, rather than accelerating and braking to keep close in line.

Use your gears properly

Engines normally deliver their most fuel-efficient performance when turning over at between 2,000 and 3,000 rpm. Above – and below – this, you are using more fuel per mile. You don't need a rev counter to tell you when you are in the zone – you should be able to tell by listening to the engine. If it's labouring, you are in too high a gear; if it's getting louder and higher pitched, you need to change up. Change up as soon as you can, and run in the highest gear that the engine can handle smoothly. A car cruising at 40 mph in fifth gear, uses 25 per cent less fuel than at the same speed in third.

Turn off when stationary

If you are likely to be stationary for more than a minute or so, turn off the engine. If the stop is less than that, switching off is not good – it will take more fuel to restart it than you would use keeping it going, and the temperature inside the catalytic converter will drop so that it does not work so efficiently, increasing the amount of pollution from your exhaust.

Don't hang about
Once you've started the engine, go. You don't need to wait for it to warm up, but do drive gently at first until the engine has reached its normal running temperature.

But take your time
The optimum speed for fuel use varies with vehicles and driving conditions but is in the range 50–60 mph. Drag increases exponentially with speed, so that by 70 mph a car can be using up to 25 per cent more fuel per mile than at 50 mph. Speeding along the motorway is illegal, but more importantly for us it is not ethical! Driving at 85 mph instead of 70 mph increases petrol consumption by 20–25 per cent.

But slower isn't necessarily more economical – 45 mph in fifth gear gives better mpg than 40 mph in fourth. Ticking over in top is the ideal speed.

Use the ventilation system
Air conditioning takes a substantial amount of power from the engine, increasing fuel consumption, and this is worse at slower speeds – according to the AA, it can add up to 11 per cent to fuel use. Open windows increase drag – and hence fuel use – and the effect is more pronounced at speed. The impact can be as much as 6 per cent. As far as possible, try to use the ventilation system alone for cooling your car.

Do you really need the car?

The most effective way to reduce your fuel consumption is to leave the car at home. About one quarter of all car journeys in the UK are of less than two miles. Could you walk or cycle instead?

Total energy costs

A car-less life may be the ethical ideal, but for most of us a car is a necessity, given our lifestyles. (And changing our lifestyles is something that we should always be willing to consider.) What car should you buy? The answer has to be the most fuel-efficient one that will meet your requirements, and this will generally be the smallest one that will do the job, and the one that offers the best mpg in its class. But this is not always the case.

Dust to dust

In 2004 and 2005, CNW Marketing Research Inc undertook a major study to try to assess the total lifetime 'dust to dust' cost of vehicles in terms of energy usage – and they really did mean 'total'. The energy costs included not only that used in the plant to manufacture the vehicle, but also the energy costs of extracting and processing the raw materials, of employees getting to work, of shipping vehicles to the dealers, of making and fitting spare parts, right through to the costs of disposal and scrapping. The costs were then worked to produce an energy cost per mile, expressed in dollars based on 2005 oil prices. There were, of course, all sorts of assumptions in calculating these figures, but the same methodology was applied throughout and this was an independent study (it was not sponsored by any sector of the automotive industry, and indeed the researchers went to some pains to ensure that the manufacturers did not realize that the study was in progress).

They identified five areas of costs:

Research and development costs are shared by all the cars built to the costed design. This can weigh heavily for experimental and specialist cars, especially if they are relatively short-lived or do below average mileage – as you will see when we look at hybrids.

Manufacturing costs are a one-off for each vehicle, but when they are shared over its lifetime and its mileage, as they are here, they become less significant the more a vehicle is used. (CNW's estimates of manufacturing costs may be on the high side. Other experts estimate these for the average car in the range of 6,000–9,000 kiloWatt hours. As the fuel energy costs are a little under 1 kWh per mile for a 40 mpg vehicle, the manufacturing costs are about the same as one year's usage.

Repair and maintenance includes the manufacture of spare parts and their shipping costs, so something which can be repaired by the local garage, using locally-sourced materials, has lower costs than one which requires replacement parts from afar.

Fuel is the petrol or diesel needed to keep it running. On an average car this represents about 80 per cent of the total lifetime energy costs.

Disposal uses less energy if the components can be recycled easily.

Some of the results were much as you might expect. The most energy expensive vehicle was the Mercedes Maybach (a 6-litre, 6-metre-long, 12-mpg limo) at $11.58 per mile; the least expensive was the Scion xB (a small Toyota, built purely for the US market) at $0.48 cents. What was more surprising at first sight – though it started to make more sense when you looked into the figures – was that the hybrids did not come out that well, in terms of overall energy consumption. For example, the conventional Honda Accord was assessed at $2.18 energy per mile, but the Hybrid version came out at $3.30 – nearly 50 per cent higher. And other hybrids/conventional comparisons showed similar pictures. Why? There are four main reasons:

- The manufacture and disposal of batteries, secondary electric motors and the power control systems – the original fitments and the replacements over the life of the vehicle – plus the use of more specialized lighter materials all require more energy.
- The hybrids are designed to perform best in town driving, and are bought mainly with that in mind. As a result, the estimated lifetime mileage of hybrids is down to around the 100,000 mark, compared to overall average of 180,000 miles.
- The current generation of hybrids are examples of developing technologies, and as such will have a relatively short life. It is likely that better, simpler, more reliable, and cheaper models will appear in the next few years, so that there will be very little second-hand use. And where vehicles are produced in limited numbers, manufacturers will not support them with spare parts for that long. CNW's researchers estimate hybrids will have a useful life of under 12 years, compared to an overall average of closer to 14.
- Research and development costs are high. A lot of energy has gone, and is still going, into the development of this new technology, and relatively few vehicles had been being produced by 2005, so that each one carried a disproportionate amount of the R&D costs. Though the development continues, the increase in sales of hybrids is reducing the relative R&D costs.

CNW are at pains to stress that hybrids are not a bad choice, it's just that, although their fuel consumption and CO_2 production may be lower, they still cost more in energy terms than some standard types of cars.

What is a hybrid?

There have been various sorts of hybrids in the past, but the modern hybrid car has electric motors (one per wheel) as well as a standard petrol or diesel engine. The electric motors draw their power from batteries which can be charged by plugging into the mains, but also charged while driving by a generator and by 'regenerative braking', which converts kinetic energy into electricity. The twin power systems, plus the sensors, switches and electronics that control it all, add to the complexity and cost of manufacturing and repair.

When used in the stop-start, slow speed conditions of town traffic, hybrids are far more fuel efficient than petrol-engined cars, delivering up to 60 mpg, compared to 30 mpg of similar-sized conventional cars. At higher speeds, hybrids use only their petrol/diesel engines, and their performance is – inevitably – no better than a conventional one. It makes sense for society to encourage the use of hybrids in town, e.g. by exempting them from the London congestion charge.

From the green perspective, one of the bonuses of hybrids is that they are becoming the new celebrity drive. The fact that Cameron Diaz, Harrison Ford, Woody Harrelson, Kurt Russell, Leonardo di Caprio, Tom Hanks and other big Hollywood names own and drive hybrids has made them fashionable in the States and elsewhere. In 2006, the Toyota Camry hybrid was the top-selling car in the USA. This is a significant step forward from the days when it seemed that all the A-list (and B-list and C-list) names were buying gas-guzzling 4x4s.

The other real surprise was that while SUV (sports utility vehicles, which we call 4x4s) may have poor fuel economy, their overall costs are not that high. For example, the Hummer H3 (a big one!) was assessed at only $1.95 per mile – lower than hybrids, and lower than the overall average of $2.28 per mile. Why? For the same reason as the poor score of the hybrids, but at the other ends of the scales:

- Simplicity of manufacture and of repair – it's mostly just metal-bashing. Reasonably competent mechanics can repair most elements and even make replacement parts.

- They clock-up high mileages – an average of 270,000 – 50 per cent more than average, nearly three times as much as a hybrid.
- They last for years – typically over 20 years' active life.
- SUVs use well-established technology, with very little new research going into them (except for marketing!), so R&D costs are tiny.

CNW's best and worst for lifetime energy efficiency

The top five:

1 Scion xB ($0.48 per mile)
2 Ford Escort ($0.57 per mile)
3 Jeep Wrangler ($0.60 per mile)
4 Chevrolet Tracker ($0.69 per mile)
5 Toyota Echo ($0.70 per mile)

The bottom five:

1 Mercedes Benz Maybach ($11.58 per mile)
2 Volkswagen Phaeton ($11.21 per mile)
3 Rolls-Royce ($10.66 per mile)
4 Bentley ($10.56 per mile)
5 Audi allroad Quattro ($5.59 per mile)

4x4s are bad for your health – and for other people's

Ask a 4x4 driver why they bought their vehicle, and they will probably tell you that their main concern was safety – especially the safety of their children – and that the key factors were the high ride, with its longer visibility and the solid coachwork. If they are telling the truth, then it is only because they are too idle or too stupid to read and understand the safety facts. Drivers and passengers of 4x4s are 6 per cent more likely to die in road accidents than occupants of standard cars. This is mainly because the high centre of gravity makes 4x4s three times more likely than standard cars to roll over, and the roofs are prone to collapse during a rollover, crushing the occupants. Drivers of 4x4s are also around twice as likely to back over their own children and kill them – around 30 children a year die this way in the US.

Big 4x4s are also more dangerous to other road-users. In side-impact collisions, where a 4x4 runs into a standard car, the car driver is 30 times more likely to be killed than the 4x4 driver; in a similar collision between standard cars, the driver who is run into is only 6.6 times more likely to be killed. The main reason for this is that 4x4s have much higher bumpers, so that instead of hitting the reinforced doors, they go through at window height.

Why do people really buy 4x4s? According to market research undertaken – though not publicized – by US car manufacturers, 4x4 buyers tend to be 'insecure and vain. They are frequently nervous about their marriages and uncomfortable about parenthood. They often lack confidence in their driving skills. Above all, they are apt to be self-centered and self-absorbed, with little interest in their neighbors and communities' (*High and Mighty: SUVs*, by Keith Bradsher).

Alternative fuels

The ideal fuels are electricity or hydrogen, as long as both are derived using renewable technology. But neither of these – as yet – is suitable for mass-market, main-use cars. We'll come back to both of them later, after we have looked at petrol, diesel and their possible alternatives.

Petrol and diesel

The combustion of petrol and diesel is a major contributor to global warming, and we should reduce our use on those grounds alone, but there is another and more commanding reason to cut down. Both are derived from crude oil, and there's a finite supply of that. Globally, oil production has probably peaked – from here on out, it's going to get scarcer and more expensive. (At the time of writing, oil is selling at $80 a barrel, up from $60 in 2006, and compared to under $20 a barrel only ten years ago.)

'It's no secret anymore that for every nine barrels of oil we consume, we are only discovering one.' *The BP Statistical Review of World Energy*

Of the two, diesel is less damaging to the environment. For the same size and make of vehicle, a diesel engine will give up to 30 per cent better fuel efficiency, produce less CO_2 (though more particulates and nitrous oxide), and last longer with fewer repairs.

Liquefied Petroleum Gas (LPG)

LPG is a mixture of propane and butane. It's a hydrocarbon, produced from natural gas and also as a by-product of refining oil (they used to flare it off in the past). LPG burns cleaner than petrol or diesel, with lower emissions of carbon dioxide, carbon monoxide, nitrous oxide and particulates. A petrol engine can be modified to run on LPG, and though this will cost something over £1,500, LPG is about half the price of petrol, so that running costs are dramatically lower. LPG gives slightly poorer performance than petrol, delivering about 7 per cent less power.

Not every filling station has an LPG facility, though the number is increasing rapidly – there are over 1,000 at the time of writing – but there's no danger of being stranded without fuel, as a converted vehicle retains its petrol tank and can still run on petrol if need be.

You can find out more about the practicalities of switching to LPG at **www.autogas.ltd.uk**, the website of AutoGas, the UK's leader in this market.

Compressed Natural Gas (CNG)

Petrol and diesel vehicles can also be converted to run on CNG, which, like LPG, is more fuel efficient and produces lower emissions. CNG is less popular, and with reason. The conversion is around twice as expensive, mainly because of the pressures involved. LPG is stored at around 125 psi (pounds per square inch), which is about four times the pressure of the air in your tyres. CNG is stored at between 2,400 and 3,600 psi. You need a much more robust tank, tougher piping and a pressure reduction system to deliver gas to the engine.

Ethanol and flexi-fuel

Ethanol is a form of alcohol produced by fermenting vegetable matter. In Brazil, the world's largest producer of ethanol, they use sugar cane as the feedstock, but any plant material – including domestic vegetable waste – can be used. It is a clear burning fuel, with a high octane rating, which delivers good efficiency. You can run cars on pure ethanol, but in Europe it is usually blended with petrol (typically 85 per cent ethanol, 15 per cent petrol) for use in 'flexi-fuel vehicles' (FFVs). Ford, Saab and Volvo are all now offering FFVs. What makes them flexible is that they can also run on pure petrol if they can't find an ethanol filling station.

As ethanol is produced from carbon dioxide-capturing vegetation, then in theory it is carbon neutral, and may be seen as a renewable energy source. The reality is slightly more complicated, and we'll get back to it when we look at bio-diesel.

Bio-diesel

Bio-diesel is a substitute for diesel produced from plant sources, such as palm oil, rape seed, and sunflowers. Like ethanol it is, in theory, carbon neutral and renewable, and cars running on it produce fewer toxic emissions – no sulphur dioxide, half as much soot and particulates, up to 50 per cent less carbon monoxide, and anything up to 95 per cent less hydrocarbons.

When Rudolph Diesel developed his 'rational heat engine' at the end of the nineteenth century, he intended it to be run on vegetable oils, and the model that he displayed at the 1900 World's Fair in Paris was fuelled by peanut oil. During most of the twentieth century, fossil oil was so cheap and plentiful that the diesel engine's vegetable roots were very largely forgotten. They were remembered again at the start of this century, and came to the public's eye in stories of cars running on chip fat – waste cooking oil can be converted into a viable fuel with very little processing. Some diesel engines can even run on pure, unprocessed vegetable oil, though they can be hard to start in winter as it is thicker than fossil diesel fuel. (If you are interested in making your own, have a look at the Collaborative Diesel Tutorial at the BioDiesel Community, **http://www.biodiesel community.org.**)

Governments have leapt on bio-diesel as a voter-friendly way to 'fight climate change', and are promoting it with a variety of tax incentives. In the UK, bio-diesel currently costs about half as much as standard diesel, and is effectively free of tax for private motorists. But there is a real question as to how far bio-diesel really is environmentally friendly, and whether it is actually carbon neutral.

The costs of bio-diesel

A US government study in 1998 looked at the energy costs of producing bio-diesel from soya – taking into account everything from tractor fuel and fertilizer production through to processing into fuel oil. They found that overall there was an output of a little over three units of fuel energy for every one unit of fossil fuel used in its production. This is a significant energy gain –

and if you substitute bio-diesel for fossil fuel in the production chain, then it becomes a sustainable energy source. And it's a far better one than bio-ethanol. (The same study showed that this had an energy yield of only 1.34 – you only get 30 per cent more energy from ethanol than goes into producing it. As ethanol/petrol engines are also less efficient than diesel ones, bio-diesel is a way to go if you are going to grow your fuel.)

Energy gain, however, is not the only consideration. You need very large areas of land to grow sufficient crops to meet the oil needs of modern economies, and the problem lies in what is being displaced from that land. If crops are grown for fuel, rather than consumption, it can increase food costs. We are already seeing this. In 2006, approximately 15 per cent of the US maize crop was taken out of the food chain and used for bio-diesel. Combined with poor harvests, the result was a major increase in the price of maize both at home and for export – in Mexico tortilla prices rose by 60 per cent, and there were riots in the streets. In the US, maize prices doubled from January 2006 to mid-2007, when the government began to promote bio-diesel as the solution to dependency on foreign oil imports. This pushed up prices right across the food sector, and increased the demand for fertilizer – maize is a hungry crop. Nitrate fertilizers are made from urea, derived from natural gas, and this is being imported from the Middle East in huge quantities.

In Europe, currently less than 1.5 per cent of fuels are bio-fuels, but an EU directive has already been agreed that will require this to rise to 5.75 per cent by 2012, and 10 per cent by 2020. You would have to turn over a quarter of Europe's arable land to fuel crops to meet these targets with locally produced bio-fuels. Which brings us to the next point.

We are exporting our problems with bio-fuels as we are with so many of our environmental problems. In Indonesia and the Philippines, large swathes of forest are being cleared for palm oil plantations, for bio-diesel production. The destruction of habitats is endangering rare plants and animal species – orang-utans face extinction – but deforestation also has a very negative impact on the carbon balance. Forests lock up carbon in their wood, and trap more of it in the humus and soil of the forest floor. Much of this is released when the land is cleared and burnt before planting with crops. In environmental terms, if you are going to clear forests to make bio-diesel, you might just as well use fossil fuel.

One hope for the future may lie in algae. Some strains of algae have up to 50 per cent oil content, and it grows much faster than higher plants. As a result, algae could yield up to 5,000 gallons per acre, per year, compared to Chinese tallow – the most productive bio-fuel crop – which yields only 700 gallons. They are still at the small scale trials stage, and there is a lot of research that still needs doing to develop a strain that will give high yields and be suitable for full-scale production. In time, this could provide a solution to our transport fuel needs, but you can't plan on possibilities. The reality is that petrol and diesel are going to be increasingly rare and expensive for the foreseeable future.

Capturing the sun's energy

Bio-diesel, like wood or any other kind of grown fuel, is a means of converting sunlight into another, more flexible form of energy. How does it compare to solar cells? In photosynthesis, plants use sunlight to combine carbon dioxide and water into hydrocarbons, and that locks in between 3 per cent and 6 per cent of the available solar energy. After you have factored in the energy inputs in growing the crop, and in processing it into bio-diesel, around 1 per cent of the sun's energy has been captured. The best solar cells can convert 15 per cent of the sunlight falling onto them into electricity – and they require virtually no maintenance or energy inputs once they have been installed. A purely rational society would build PV arrays rather than bio-diesel crops, but society doesn't take the decisions – farmers do. And what they see is that rape or sunflowers require little capital investment, and there is a good market for them.

Fuel cells

The technology of fuel cells is very complex. For our purposes, it is enough to know that in the best types of fuel cell, hydrogen and oxygen are combined over a catalyst to produce electricity, and the only waste products are heat and water – both of which can be disposed of with no bother. There are other types of fuel cell, including those which combine petrol and air to produce electricity – with carbon dioxide and water as their wastes. (And if you want to really understand fuel cells, go to **www.howstuffworks.com** or **www.wikipedia.com** – either site will give you a good technical explanation.)

Fuel cells can be used wherever electricity is needed, but probably their most important use nowadays is as the 'engine' in cars. A fuel cell system of about the same size as an internal combustion engine will deliver enough electricity to power a car. And it will deliver more miles per gallon! If you feed hydrogen into a fuel cell, then at best about 60 per cent of its available energy will be converted into mechanical energy to drive the car forwards. In a hydrogen-powered internal combustion engine, only around 20 per cent of the potential energy of the hydrogen is converted into mechanical energy – there is a huge loss in the form of heat, and in powering the fans and pumps that are needed to control the heat. (The differences are less marked with petrol-powered fuel cells and internal combustion engines, because there is a loss of power in converting petrol for fuel cell use.)

So why don't we all use fuel cell cars? In 2007, the answer is that they are not yet on sale – but production models are expected soon. They will almost certainly be more expensive than the equivalent conventional car, but should be cheaper to run – mainly because they use fuel more efficiently, but there will also be tax and congestion charge benefits.

Hydrogen is the most efficient and cleanest fuel for fuel cells, but it's not the most convenient. The main problem is storage – you have to compress or liquefy it to fit a viable quantity into a reasonable space. There are currently three possible solutions: very high pressure tanks; liquefaction at ultra-low temperature (-253°C) – and it takes a lot of energy to keep things that cold; and tanks containing special alloys which can absorb hydrogen under pressure, and release it as required. The latter is the safest solution, but it makes for heavy tanks.

The more practical alternative is to use a liquid fuel from which hydrogen can be generated easily. Petrol, natural gas, ethanol, methanol and propane are all possibilities, but the best is methanol as it needs the least processing. Environmentally, the catch is that this also produces CO_2 as a waste product – as do all the alternatives.

Electric (battery) cars

Battery-powered electric cars have been touted as the answer to urban transport for many years, but have only really taken off in the last couple of years. Tax incentives in several countries, such as exemption from London's congestion charge, have stimulated the market, and improvements in battery design mean that electric cars are a practical alternative to internal combustion ones for city driving. Modern electric cars, like the G-Wiz, can zip around through traffic with the same acceleration as most normal cars. (And the top speed of around 45 mph is not a problem in town.) An overnight charge costs around 40p (at off-peak rates) and will power the car for up to 40 miles – that's right, about 1p a mile! Compare that to petrol/diesel cars, where the best will cost you 8p a mile at current prices. If you use a standard electricity supplier, their CO_2 emissions are rated at about 60 gms per km – a little over half of the lowest-rated diesel cars. And if you use a green electricity supplier, there are zero emissions.

Electric cars are not without environmental impact – batteries pose the biggest problem. A standard battery has a life of three years, after which it must be replaced and disposed of. The electric car vendors run recycling schemes, but there are still some quite nasty chemicals in there that someone has to deal with. There is a new generation of lithium batteries just coming onto the market. These promise twice the lifespan, twice the power storage, and simpler disposal.

Most of the electric cars currently on the market are designed to be one-person run-arounds. They will take a second person and the shopping, but not much more – ideal for commuters, but not a practical family vehicle. The Mega City also comes in a 2+2 version, which could take the children (while they are small).

At first sight, electric cars can seem to be expensive compared to other small cars. They cost upwards of £8,000 new and the batteries will set you back £1,500 every three years. Against that, you have a running cost saving of at least 7p per mile, no congestion charge or road tax (and cheap/free parking in London). In London, an electric car can pay for itself completely in a couple of years – mainly because of the congestion charge exemption and parking concessions. Elsewhere, an electric car is not the cheapest solution to urban travel, though it is the greenest.

figure 8.2 The striking Elettrica – sharply styled, but comfortingly safe with its aluminium safety cage and all-round visibility. At the time of writing, this is the only electric car available with Lithium batteries, which offer a 70-mile range, a ten-year lifespan and a better performance than conventional lead acid batteries.

For more information:

GoingGreen, main agents for G-Wiz:

www.goingreen.co.uk

Nice Car Company, agents for the Mega City (also sell electric trucks and bikes):

www.nicecarcompany.co.uk

Future Vehicles, sell the Elettrica, which boasts Italian styling and a high safety specification:

www.futurevehicles.co.uk

Which car?

If you decide that you do need a car, which one is right for you? Focus on how the car will be used most of the time.

- How many people will normally be travelling in it?
- How much luggage will it be carrying?
- How often will it be used to transport bulky loads?

Remember the mantra:

- **Small is beautiful** – Pick the smallest car that will do the job most of the time.
- **Least is best** – And sometimes *leased* is best. If you only need a large vehicle a few times a year, then perhaps you should buy a small one and hire a large one when needed. The regular savings on fuel, insurance, tax and maintenance can pay for the hire charges.
- **Use and reuse** – Do you need a new car? Can you continue to use your existing one longer? Will a second-hand car do the job just as well? The more use that you can get out of anything – including cars – the better it is for the environment. (Though the exception here is that older vehicles may well be much more polluting that modern ones. Sometimes they need to be taken off the road! Your garage will give you an emissions reading when they do the MOT.)

Once you have decided on the type, there are several services on the web that will tell you the greenest of that type, and/or give you detailed figures of selected models. CO_2 emission levels and mpg figures are the two obvious measures of 'greenness', but they are not the only factors. The environmental impact of the car's construction is also an issue – for example, how much recycled material is used in making it and how easily can it be recycled at the end of its life. What Green Car (**www.whatgreencar.com**) includes fuel, emissions and the vehicle life cycle in its assessments to produce their guide to greener car buying.

In autumn 2007, these were their top recommendations in the city-car, supermini, small family, large family, convertible and multi-purpose vehicle classes. They also cover larger cars, but cars built for status or recreation just can't be green.

Rating	Make and Model	Fuel	CO_2 emissions	mpg
City cars				
1	Nice MEGA City	Green electric		
Supermini				
1	VW Polo Blue Motion 1.4 TDi	Diesel	99	74.3
Small family car				
1	Vauxhall Astra 1.4i	LPG		
Large family car				
1	Toyota Pirus Mark 11	Petrol hybrid	104	65
Convertible				
1	Smart Fortwo Cabrio	Petrol	113	60.1
Multi-purpose vehicle				
1	Vauxhall Mervia 1.3 CTDi	Diesel	135	56.5

figure 8.3 What Green Car has a comprehensive database of car models. Check out their Top 10 for the class of vehicle that you need. And look around the site while you are there – there's lots of high-quality information and advice at **www.whatgreencar.com**.

Useful websites

VCA Car fuel data – will give you emission level, mpg figures and other details for any current and recent car models – www.vcacarfueldata.org.uk

Find a car – the US government fuel economy site that has fuel usage and other data for vehicles back to 1985. You may not find an old British or European car there, and the mpg figures are based on US gallons (multiply by 1.2 to convert to UK mpg) – http://www.fueleconomy.gov/feg/findacar.htm

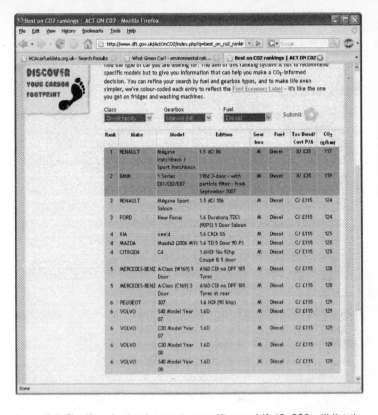

figure 8.4 The 'Best in class' page at **www.dft.gov.uk/ActOnCO2** will list the cars with the lowest CO₂ emissions. From the drop-down lists, select the class, the gearbox type (manual or automatic) and the fuel. Click 'Submit' and the best ten will appear, in rank order.

ETA (Environmental Transport Association) promotes greener motoring, cycle use and other issues – **http://www.eta.co.uk/**

BoostLPG promotes the use of LPG fuel, with details of installers and service stations – an essential resource for anyone thinking of converting to LPG – **http://www.boostlpg.com/**

The Energy Saving Trust's Efficient Driving page – how to get more miles per gallon – **http://www.energysavingtrust. org.uk/what_can_i_do_today/efficient_driving**

The Green Car Site – for specifications, reviews and links to vendors across the whole range of green vehicles – http://www.greencarsite.co.uk

Summary

- The use of petrol and diesel for motoring is one of the major causes of the increase in greenhouse gases, and a key factor in climate change. We must use dramatically less.
- Take the time to look at just how you use your car, and decide whether you really need one.
- If you must use a car, use it efficiently. Keep it properly maintained and adjust your driving to minimize fuel use.
- The total energy used by a car over its lifetime includes that which goes into its manufacturing, maintenance and repair as well as that used on the road.
- Petrol and diesel are not the only fuels. Alternatives include LPG, ethanol, bio-diesel and electricity, from fuel cells or batteries.
- Bio-fuels do not offer a simple solution, as their production poses environmental and ethical problems.
- Electric cars are getting much better. They are a viable, economical solution to city motoring.
- When buying a new car, assess your needs carefully, and go for the smallest and most fuel-efficient that will meet your normal needs.

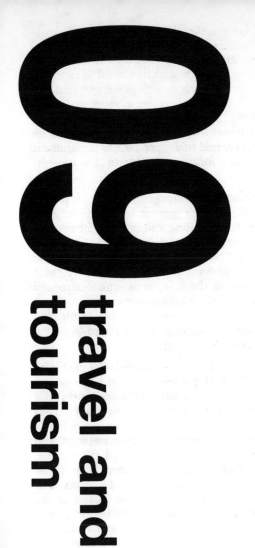

09

travel and tourism

In this chapter you will learn:

- how air travel contributes to global warming
- about carbon-offset schemes
- how tourism can be bad for the environment
- about ecotourism and sustainable tourism.

Air travel

Over the last half century, air travel has grown more than twice as fast as average economic growth, and this trend is expected to continue into the foreseeable future, with passenger numbers set to double by 2020. Currently, air travel is estimated to be responsible for about 5 per cent of the world's greenhouse gas emissions – as much as is generated by all human activity in Africa! This is projected to triple to 15 per cent by 2050 as air travel increases while other forms of pollution are brought under control.

Flight is the most environmentally damaging form of travel. A round trip from the UK to Australia generates – per passenger – as much CO_2 as is produced in heating and lighting the average house for a whole year. And it's not just CO_2. Aircraft also produce nitrogen oxides (NOx) and water vapour – which you can often see as contrails across the sky – and these have twice the global warning impact of the CO_2 emissions. Short-haul flights are proportionately worse (it takes more energy to get up than to stay up). Compared to using the car (with one occupant), flying is five times as damaging; compared to taking the train, it does ten times more damage.

The UK's airports are among the world's busiest, second only to those of the USA. One fifth of all passenger flights begin or end in the UK. The UK is therefore crucial to how the world as a whole tackles the environmental impact of air travel. It is unfortunate, to say the least, that current government policy is to encourage expansion of the industry – new runways and terminals are planned, and air travel is subsidized through the tax system. Air Passenger Duty is charged, but there is no tax on aviation fuel and no VAT on plane tickets. If fuel was taxed at the same rate as car fuel, and VAT charged on tickets at the usual rate, this would bring in an estimated £10 billion a year, compared to less than £1 billion on Air Passenger Duty – in effect the Treasury is subsidizing air travel to the tune of £9 billion a year. (A fair rate of tax on flights would add to their costs, but it would save every taxpayer over £200 a year.)

Carbon-offset schemes

Carbon offsetting is presented as the guilt-free way to fly. The theory is simple. When you are booking your flight, you pay a little extra which will be contributed to a project that will in some way reduce the amount of CO_2 in the atmosphere by the same amount that your flight will put into it. And voila, carbon-neutral flying! It's the same principle that is used in emissions trading, where large-scale polluters buy into reforestation, renewable energy development or similar schemes.

There have been some doubts about these.

One of the key requirements is that the scheme would not happen without the money from carbon offsetting – if a government or other organization was going to make the investment anyway, it does not count, because all you have done is reduced the costs to the developer.

Another requirement is that the scheme should have environmental benefits – which may sound obvious, but things are not always clear cut. Take tree planting. Tree-planting schemes are much favoured by carbon offsetters because we all know that growing trees absorb carbon, and they look green and we associate woods and forests with nature. Generally, they are valid. Reforesting an area, by replanting it with native trees, is in most cases a good thing to do. However, it can be ecologically damaging to plant trees where previously there had been grassland or heath, or to plant quick-growing (so they have a higher carbon-grabbing value) firs or eucalyptus instead of native trees.

Finally, there have been questions about how the money really is spent. How much, if any, of your carbon-offset money actually went into planting trees, or providing solar-powered ovens? How much went onto office overheads, organizational costs, legitimate profits or simple fraud? Even where the company that sells the carbon offset is well-motivated and well-organized, with minimal overheads, how far are they able to monitor what is actually happening at the scheme in Panama or Liberia? (And most carbon-offset schemes are located in developing countries because it is much cheaper to save carbon there than it is in the West.)

At the time of writing, the government was still trying to establish a certification system for these schemes. The best that is currently available is that of Certified Emission Reduction credits, based on the Kyoto carbon trading market and the UN's Clean Development Mechanism – though some projects approved under that have been shown to be ineffective. It's interesting that the Co-op's travel business, Travelcare, having announced its carbon-offset facility at the start of 2007, had abandoned it by the end of the same year.

Of the various carbon-offset organizations currently around, the following may be worth a closer look:

co2balance (www.co2balance.uk.com) runs its own offsetting projects, mainly overseas, and guarantees that these are all projects that are fully additional, transparent and verified.

Treeflights (www.treeflights.com) have their own planting schemes in Wales and in the Amazon.

Erase my Footprint (www.erasemyfootprint.com) runs independently-audited tree-planting schemes in Devon and Cornwall, for offsetting carbon from flights, driving and other domestic or business activities.

Climate Care (www.climatecare.org) runs a variety of projects in the UK and overseas, and has earned a good reputation for sustainability.

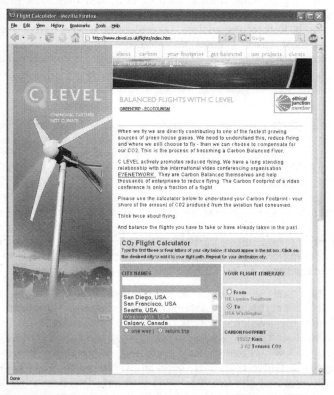

figure 9.1 At C Level, the aim is to reduce flying, and their main target is business travel. When you go to their site to calculate and offset your carbon, you will be encouraged to think about videoconferencing as an alternative to travelling.

Must-do

- Support any campaigns against new runways and for taxes on flights.
- Fly less, or stop flying altogether.

Worth doing

- **Take the train** – At one-tenth of the CO_2 emissions of a flight, this is the most environmentally friendly way to travel. Eurostar will take you from London to Paris at an environmental cost of 5.5 kg of CO_2 – a flight would cost 50 kg. City centre to city centre, and with minimal or no check-in delays, the train can also be quicker over distances of up to 500 kms or so.
- **Switch to virtual business meetings** – Teleconferencing is a practical alternative to travel for business meetings. Presentations and documents can be shared and worked on collaboratively through internet connections – with very little special equipment, software or skills.
- **If you must fly, offset** – It will make you feel better, and if you choose one with worthwhile projects, it will do some good.

Tourism

Most forms of tourism are environmentally damaging. We burn up oil by the air mile getting there; stay in concrete hotels that took large quantities of energy and resources to build and continue to take energy and resources to run; we play golf on courses that have wiped out eco-systems and draw masses of water from dwindling rivers and reservoirs; we destroy the local culture and replace it with standard holiday facilities; the tour operators and hotel chains employ locals on minimum wages and export the profits back to the West. It doesn't have to be this way.

Ecotourism

Ecotourism has been the fastest-growing sector of the tourism industry over the last few years, and now accounts for around 5 per cent of all holidays. It's an unfortunate fact that many of the environmentally aware, ecologically-oriented holidays are in distant lands, so there are a lot of air miles travelled in reaching them – which creates something of a dilemma.

Ecotourism is environmentally-friendly travel – going to natural areas in a way that helps to protect the environment and improves the lot of the local inhabitants. More specifically, to count as ecotourism a holiday should:

- have little impact on the environment, with low-tech and/or carbon-neutral accommodation and minimal use of powered transport
- involve activities which conserve or restore the local ecological balance
- maximize the benefits to the local community, by using locally-owned hotels and other facilities
- be sensitive to the local culture, and be developed with the active participation of the local population
- be sustainable.

Some activities that are promoted as ecotourism hardly meet these criteria, and the 'eco' label is not much more than 'greenwashing' (making things appear to be more environmentally friendly than they really are). You will find, for example, safaris labelled 'ecotourism' that involve internal flights, extensive 4x4 driving and accommodation in (energy-intensive) luxury hotels.

Ecotourism is used by many countries to help finance the protection of the natural environment. For most, it is a fairly marginal activity, but there are some where ecotourism makes a very significant contribution to the total economy. These include Costa Rica, Ecuador, Kenya, Madagascar and Nepal. Costa Rica is the world leader in ecotourism, thanks to two major advantages – an incredible diversity of wildlife, and promixity to the United States, the world's leading exporter of tourists. Ecotourism has helped to preserve the rainforests and highlands from destructive development – national parks make up 28 per cent of Costa Rica; it has brought additional monies, in the form of jobs and small-scale projects, to remote areas, supporting the local economy and society; it has ensured that most tourist income goes into local pockets (in large-scale tourist developments, funded by outside investment, most of the profits are sent out of the country). The large number of visitors (over 1 million last year) is having some impact on the parks – trails are being eroded, animals are becoming used to human contact – but the alternatives of logging and clearance for plantations would have been far worse.

figure 9.2 The Earthwatch Institute runs scientific expeditions and projects with the focus on the environment and sustainability. What they offer are 'holidays' in the sense that you are taken somewhere different and pay for the privilege, but you will also do something useful – and probably meet some interesting people and have a fascinating time. Find out more at **www.earthwatchexpeditions.org**.

Sustainable tourism

'Take nothing but pictures, leave nothing but footprints and waste nothing but time.'

Sustainable tourism aims to preserve the local environment, society and economy, so that future tourists can enjoy them and so that the locals continue to get a benefit from tourism. It's about working with the local people to provide low-impact activities, low-energy accommodation, and low-carbon travel, and ensuring that a large part of the profits stay in the local area.

The most sustainable tourism, of course, is that which requires the least travel. Holidays in the UK, or those reached by ferry and car on the nearer parts of the continent, must be better. A holiday which involves little travel once you have arrived will also be better. In fact, the most environmentally responsible holidays are probably the ones like those that most people took in the not too distant past – by train to the seaside.

Green Tourism is a UK accreditation scheme for hotels, guest houses, caravan parks, campsites and other forms of accommodation, which meet the required standards of environmental awareness, energy efficiency, recycling, etc. Members of the scheme can be recognized by the logo on their websites and brochures.

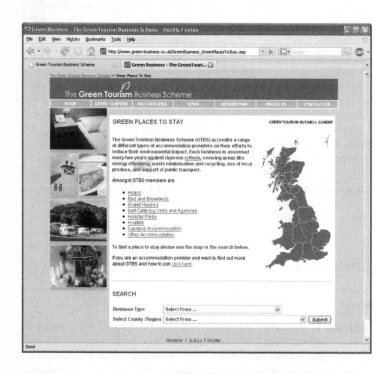

figure 9.3 You can avoid the whole 'Will carbon offsetting justify my flight?' question by taking your holidays in the UK, and you can cut your environmental impact still further by taking a green holiday. See what's on offer at **www.green-business.co.uk**.

Tourism sites

Ethical Escape – www.ethicalescape.com

A directory of low-impact/zero-carbon accommodation in the UK, Europe and beyond.

Responsible travel – www.responsibletravel.com

Sustainable and eco-friendly holidays.

figure 9.4 Responsible travel is a UK-based specialist in eco-friendly and sustainable tourism, offering a wide choice of destinations and styles of holiday, from budget camping, through adventure holidays, to luxury hotels, all with at least some green credentials, and all rated by past customers. Visit them at **www.responsibletravel.com**.

Exodus – www.exodus.co.uk

Offers small-group, low-impact, exploration and adventure holidays.

International Ecotourism Society – www.ecotourism.org

A central resource for people interested in ecotourism, as organizers, researchers and activists, but also a good place to look for holidays.

Green tourism in Scotland – www.greentourism.org.uk

Green tourism in the Isle of Wight – www.greenisland tourism.org

Green tourism in Devon – www.greentourismadvice.co.uk

Must-do

- Give the planet a break. Resist the lures of cheap weekend flights to Dublin, Barcelona and Rome. If you want to get away for the weekend, take the train – there are lots of interesting places in the UK, and Paris is only two and a half hours from central London nowadays.
- Give yourself a break from driving. Even if you have to use the car to get there, aim to keep out of the car as far as possible while you are on holiday. Walk and cycle to get around – you don't have to be anywhere in a hurry because you are on holiday.

Worth doing

- Choose locally-owned, low-impact accommodation in preference to high-rise, high maintenance hotels owned by international chains.
- Think about ecotourism for your next holiday (preferably at a destination you can reach without flying).

Summary

- Air travel contributes significantly to global warning, and its contribution is growing rapidly at a time when other forms of CO_2 emission are being reduced.
- It is difficult to assess the real value of carbon-offset schemes.
- Tourism can be very damaging to the environment in general, and to the local environments and communities in tourist destinations.
- Ecotourism is more sensitive to local eco-systems and cultures.
- Sustainable or responsible tourism has lower environmental impact.
- We all need to fly less, and drive less.

taking it further

At home

Get your family on board. Agree some short-term and long-term targets, and the steps you will take to get to them. Make sure everyone has their own part to play.

Once you feel you have made some significant lifestyle changes, go back to whichever site you used, in Chapter 01, to work out your ecological footprint and reassess yourself. How much difference have you made? How much more could you do?

Weigh your waste. For a full week, weigh your rubbish bags before you put them out, and add them up to find the total weight. The following week, try to ensure that anything which can be kept for reuse, sent to recycling, or put into the compost, goes to its proper place and not in the rubbish. Weigh the bags, as before. How much less rubbish is there? Over the next two weeks, make a special effort to avoid over-packaging, and to minimize food waste. Keep weighing those bags! You should be able to reduce your waste by half, without too much effort. If you can comfortably get it down further, do so, then stick to your new-found habits.

If you haven't got an energy meter, read your electricity meter at the same time each week for a month, and work out the previous week's usage. See how far you can reduce this, week by week. And get the family involved! You all need to be turning off unwanted lights and appliances, and wearing warmer clothes.

At work

Is your organization already recycling and reducing waste? If not, see if you can get things moving. Head for the Waste at Work section of Waste Online at **www.wasteonline.org.uk** where you will find advice on how to start and links to recycling companies and organizations.

What could you do to reduce your organization's energy use? Could you start a 'Turn down, turn off' campaign to encourage others to turn down thermostats and turn off unused lights, PCs and other appliances?

In larger organizations, there may be opportunities for car-sharing among employees. If it is big enough, it may be worth thinking about a bespoke database – contact National Car Share at **www.nationalcarshare.co.uk**. Otherwise, encourage people to join a local car-share scheme – find the ones in your area through **www.carshare.com**.

In your community

How green is your council? What is it doing to promote reduced car use, energy efficiency, renewable energy development, recycling, and waste reduction? Where does it need a push? Get involved, whether that means contacting your councillor, joining a local green campaigning group or one of the parties, or standing for the council.

What local recycling facilities are there? Are they enough? People will use bottle banks and other resource collectors more readily if they are more accessible. If you feel more are needed, talk to the recycling officer at your local council.

If you have children at school, how do they get there? Does the school run 'walking buses'? Does it provide secure cycle racks? Are there safe cycle routes to the school? Talk to the school. They should have a transport policy that aims to reduce car use. And if they don't, ask them why not.

What could you do to support one or more local or national charities in the green or fairtrade areas?

index

4x4 vehicles **159–60**

A lot of organics website **134**
About Organics website **126**
air fresheners **62**
air miles **83–4, 101**
air pollution **148–9**
air travel **174–7**
algae **164**
animal rights **3**
animal welfare **98–9**
antibacterial chemicals **69**
asimpleswitch website *35*
AutoGas website **161**

bag-free towns **133**
baking soda **63, 67–8**
bamboo **123**
Bamboo Clothes website **123**
bananas, and fairtrade **113**
banking **140–3**
baths **31, 61**
battery cars **165–7**
Best Foot Forward website **9**
bicarbonate of soda **63, 67–8**
BigBarn website *88*
bio-diesel **162–3**
bio-fuels **102, 161–4**
BioDiesel Community website **162**
boilers **21–3**
BoostLPG website **171**
bottled water **114–15**
building societies **144**
Burma **3**

Buy Nothing Day website **118**
buying decisions **2–4**

C Level website *176*
Calch Ty-Mawr Lime (Welsh Centre
        for Traditional and Ecological
        Building) website **21**
car sharing **185**
carbon dioxide (CO_2)
    air travel emissions **174**
    car emissions **148–9,** *171*
    food chain emissions *82,* **102**
    levels **6**
    lifetime costs **7–8**
    and oil **15**
    and patio heaters **28**
    savings **7–8, 35**
carbon footprint **10,** *11*
carbon offsetting **174–6**
carpeting **79**
cars
    4x4 vehicles **159–60**
    alternative fuels **160–5**
    choice of **168–9**
    and CO_2 emissions **148,** *171*
    costs **149–51**
    electric **165–7**
    and ethical choices **3**
    hybrid **3, 7, 157–8**
    lifetime energy cost **156**
    manufacture **152**
    reducing costs **152–5**
    SUVs (sports utility vehicles)
            158–9

Cartridge Express website 55
Cartridge World website 56
Cash for Cartridges website 55
catalytic converters 149
cavity wall insulation 19, 20
CFL bulbs 33–4, 35
Charity Bank 143
charity shops 123
chimenea 28
choices, ethical 2–4
CIS (Co-operative Insurance
      Sustainable) Leaders Trust
      145
clay paints 73
cleaning
   materials 69–70
   products 62–9
Climate Care website 176
clothes 119–26
cloths 69–70
CNG (compressed natural gas) 161
Co-operative Bank 140–1
Co-operative Insurance Sustainable
      (CIS) Leaders Trust 145
Co-operative travel business 175
CO₂ (carbon dioxide)
   air travel emissions 174
   car emissions 148–9, 171
   food chain emissions 82, 102
   levels 6
   lifetime costs 7–8
   and oil 15
   and patio heaters 28
   savings 7–8, 35
CO₂balance website 176
coal 15
community, sense of 11–12
companies 4–5
composting 102, 104–7
compressed natural gas (CNG) 161
computers 53–4
Computers for Charity website 54
condensing boilers 22
consumption decisions 2–4
cookers 41–2
cooking 40–2
cooking oil 103
corporate greed 5
cost, of ethical living 10

Costa Rica 178
cotton 120–1

decision making 2–4
deforestation 163
diesel 160
dishwashers 48
disposable cleaning materials 69–70
disposal
   electrical appliances 57–8
   paints and varnishes 72–3
donation-giving 130
double glazing 22, 27–8
draught proofing 19, 21
dyes 121

Earth Day Footprint quiz 9
Earth Energy website 26
EarthBorn paints website 74
Earthwatch Institute website 179
Eat the seasons website 92
eco-friendly products 63–7
eco-gadgets 126–7
Eco heat pumps website 26
Eco Merchant website 21
ecoballs® 68, 69
ecological footprint 8–10
Ecology Building Society 144
ecotourism 177–9
ecover website 65–6
Efergy home CO₂ meter 56, 57
EIRIS (Ethical Investment Research
      Services) 145
elbow grease 68
electric cars 165–7
electrical appliances 45–6, 56–8
   see also individual appliances
electricity 15, 35–9
electricity usage monitors 56
electronic equipment 51–3
Elettrica car 167
embodied carbon 8
embodied energy 8
emissions trading 175
energy
   and food production 81–5
   meters 56
   sources 14–16
   use in the home 18

energy saving
  light bulbs **33–4,** *35*
  space heating **18–30**
Energy Saving Trust website *29–30,*
  171
Energy Watch website **17**
Environmental Business Products
  Ltd website **54,** *55*
environmental issues **5–6**
Environmental Transport Association
  (ETA) **170**
Environmental Transport Association
  website **149,** *151*
Erase my Footprint website **176**
ETA (Environmental Transport
  Association) **170**
ethanol **161–2**
ethical behaviour, definition of **2**
ethical companies **4–5**
Ethical Company Organisation **134**
Ethical Consumer magazine **138**
Ethical Escape website **181**
ethical investment **144–5**
Ethical Investment Association **145**
Ethical Investment Research
  Services (EIRIS) **145**
Ethical Investors Group **145**
ethical retailers **134–8**
Ethical Superstore website *128*
EU Eco-label **64**
EU energy labels **45–6**
Exodus website **182**
exploitation **5, 119**
  see also fairtrade

factory farming **98–9**
Fair Flowers Fair Plants initiative
  131
fair wages **119**
fairtrade
  food **3, 87, 110–14**
  gifts **129**
Fairtrade Foundation **111, 113,** *114*
Faith in Nature website *137,* **138**
Fareshare website **103**
farm shops **93**
farmers' markets **93,** *94*
fashion **124**
fertilizers **99, 100**

FFVs (flexi-fuel vehicles) **161**
financial advisors **145**
financial investment **144–5**
Firebelly Stoves website *24*
fish **98–9**
flax **20, 123**
flexi-fuel **161–2**
flexi-fuel vehicles (FFVs) **161**
floor coverings **78–9**
floors **78–9**
flowers **131**
fluorescent tubes **33–4**
food
  fairtrade **3, 87, 110–14**
  organic **99–101**
  packaging **108–10**
  production **81–5**
  seasonal **88–92**
  waste **102–8**
Food Climate Research Network
  website *86*
food miles **83–9, 101**
Forest Stewardship Council (FSC)
  75, *76*
4x4 vehicles **159–60**
Freecycle group **58, 77,** *78*
freezers **49–51, 57**
fridges **49–51, 57**
Friends Provident **144**
FSC (Forest Stewardship Council)
  75, *76*
fuel cells **164–5**
fuel economy website **170**
fuel miles **83–9**
fuels, alternative **160–5**
furniture **75–8**
Future Vehicles website **167**

G-Wiz electric car **166, 167**
gadgets **126–7**
gas **15**
gas boilers **22**
gas hobs **42**
Get ethical website **136**
gifts **129**
GoingGreen website **167**
Good Shopping Guide **134**
gooshing website **134,** *135*
Great Food Swap report **85**

green-business website *180*
Green Car Site **171**
green cleaning products **63–7**
Green Consumer Guide website *51*
green energy **16–17**
green helpline website **17**
Green Providers Directory **134**
Green Tourism **180, 182**
Greener Living website **136**
greenhouse gases **6, 15**
    see also CO_2 (carbon dioxide)
GreenSteps website **21**
'greenwashing' **63, 178**
growing vegetables **96–7**
growth hormones **99**
Guide me green website **134**

H_2O batteries **126, 127**
habitat destruction **163**
heat loss **19**
heat pumps **24–6**
hemp **20, 121,** *122*
herbicides **99**
hobs *41,* **42**
hot water tanks **31**
hothouse production **89**
House of Hemp website *122*
house plants **63**
household cleaners **63–9**
household waste **70–1, 184**
human aspects **11–12**
hybrid cars **3, 7, 157–8**
hydrogen **164–5**

Ice Energy website **26**
induction hobs *41,* **42**
Inetec **102**
ink cartridges **54–6**
insulation **8, 19–21, 31**
International Ecotourism Society
    182
internet banking **142**
investment **144–5**
Islamic banking **143**

kettles **42–3**

Labour Behind the Label website
    119

leather **76**
Legionnaires disease **31**
lemon juice **67**
Let's Clean Up Fashion website *120*
lifetime carbon costs **7–8**
lifetime energy costs **6–7**
light bulbs **33–4,** *35*
lighting **33**
linen **123**
linoleum **79**
liquefied petroleum gas (LPG) **161,
    171**
lithium batteries **166**
loan-giving **130**
locally grown food **87,** *88*
loft insulation *19,* **20**
low carbon building programme **30**
LPG (liquefied petroleum gas) **161,
    171**
Lucas, Caroline **85**

maize crops **163**
manufacturing energy **45**
Marine Conservation Society **98**
materials **120–3**
Maternity Exchange website **124**
meat **81–3, 98–9**
Mega City electric car **167**
methane **82–3, 102**
microfibre cloths **70**
microwave ovens **41**
milk **109–10**
money **140–6**
mortgages **144**

National Car Share website **185**
natural cleaning substances **67–8**
Natural Collection **134**
natural insulations **20–1**
natural paints **73–4**
newspaper, as insulation **20**
Nice Car Company website **167**
nitrates **100**
Norwich & Peterborough Building
    Society **144**
nuclear power **15, 16**

oil **15**
oil companies **4–5**

oil production 160
organic cotton 121
organic food 99–101
ovens 41
Owl electricity monitor 56
Oxfam 130

packaging 108–10
paints 71–4
PAN (Pesticide Action Network) 121
paper towels 69
patio heaters 28
People Tree 137
Pesticide Action Network (PAN) 121
pesticides 99, 100
petrol 160
photovoltaic (PV) cells 35–9
plant watering 61
plastic bags 131–3
pollutants 62
pollution 15, 76, 148–9
polyester fleece 123
printers 54–6
PV (photovoltaic) cells 35–9
PV-Web website *40*

radioactive waste 16
Recycle Now website *106*
recycling
  clothing 123–4
  electrical appliances 57–8
  household waste 70–1
  ink cartridges 54–6
  packaging 110
  paints and solvents 71
renewable energy 6, 15, 30
Responsible Travel website 181,
  181
retailers 134–8
road miles 84–5
room thermostats 21
rubber flooring 79

seasonal food 88–92
secondary glazing *19*
shareholder action 146
sheep's wool 20
shopping bags 131–3
shopping guides 134–8

showers 31, 61
Smile (internet bank) 142
sodium bicarbonate 63, 67–8
Soil Association 99
solar cells 35–9, 164
solar water heating 31–2
solvents 72
space heating 18–30
sponges 70
sports utility vehicles (SUVs) 158–9
stainless steel 76
standby mode 52
stewardship 5
Stove Centre website *24*
Stoves Are Us website *24*
style 124
Style Will Save Us website *125*
supermarkets 84–5, 109, 119,
  131–2
sust-it website *49*
sustain website *97*
sustainability 6
Sustainable Building Supplies
  website *21*
sustainable tourism 179–80
SUVs (sports utility vehicles) 158–9
switching websites 17

tanning (leather) 76
taps 61
teleconferencing 177
TerraPlana 137
textiles 121–3
The Ethical Living Company 137
thermostats 19, 21
timber 75, *76*
toilets 61
toner cartridges 54–6
Toner Top-up website 56
tourism 177–83
trains 177
travel 174–83
  see also cars
Travelcare 175
treeflights website 176
Triadcraft website *129*
Tridos bank 143
tumble driers 47
tyres 153

uPVC window frames **28**
usage energy **45–6**
uSwitch website **17**

varnishes **71–4**
VCA car fuel data website **170**
veg box schemes website *96*
vegan diets **101–2**
vegetables
  grow your own **96–7**
  local **93–6**
  in season **90–2**
vegetarianism **102**
vinegar **67**
VOCs (volatile organic compounds)
  62, 71–2

Wainwright Bank & Trust Company
  143
washing machines **47**
waste
  food **102–8**
  household **70–1, 184**
  radioactive **16**
waste management systems **102**
Waste Online **185**

water
  bottled **114–15**
  heating **31–2**
  use **60–1**
water meters **61**
water-powered batteries **126, 127**
WEE (Waste Electrical and
    Electronic) directive **54**
Welsh Centre for Traditional and
    Ecological Building (Calch
    Ty-Mawr Lime) website **21**
What Green Car website *170*
What's Mine Is Yours website **124**
white spirit **72**
wind turbines **6–7**
windows **21–2, 28**
wood boilers **23,** *24*
wood stoves **23,** *24,* **28**
wooden floorboards **78**
wooden furniture **75,** *76*
wool **20**
Worm City website *107*
wormeries **105–7**
WRAP website *108,* **110**

teach yourself®

From Advanced Sudoku to Zulu, you'll find everything you need in the **teach yourself** range, in books, on CD and on DVD.

Visit **www.teachyourself.co.uk** for more details.

Advanced Sudoku and Kakuro
Afrikaans
Alexander Technique
Algebra
Ancient Greek
Applied Psychology
Arabic
Arabic Conversation
Aromatherapy
Art History
Astrology
Astronomy
AutoCAD 2004
AutoCAD 2007
Ayurveda
Baby Massage and Yoga
Baby Signing
Baby Sleep
Bach Flower Remedies
Backgammon
Ballroom Dancing
Basic Accounting
Basic Computer Skills
Basic Mathematics
Beauty
Beekeeping
Beginner's Arabic Script
Beginner's Chinese Script
Beginner's Dutch

Beginner's French
Beginner's German
Beginner's Greek
Beginner's Greek Script
Beginner's Hindi
Beginner's Hindi Script
Beginner's Italian
Beginner's Japanese
Beginner's Japanese Script
Beginner's Latin
Beginner's Mandarin Chinese
Beginner's Portuguese
Beginner's Russian
Beginner's Russian Script
Beginner's Spanish
Beginner's Turkish
Beginner's Urdu Script
Bengali
Better Bridge
Better Chess
Better Driving
Better Handwriting
Biblical Hebrew
Biology
Birdwatching
Blogging
Body Language
Book Keeping
Brazilian Portuguese

Bridge
British Citizenship Test, The
British Empire, The
British Monarchy from Henry VIII, The
Buddhism
Bulgarian
Bulgarian Conversation
Business French
Business Plans
Business Spanish
Business Studies
C++
Calculus
Calligraphy
Cantonese
Caravanning
Car Buying and Maintenance
Card Games
Catalan
Chess
Chi Kung
Chinese Medicine
Christianity
Classical Music
Coaching
Cold War, The
Collecting
Computing for the Over 50s
Consulting
Copywriting
Correct English
Counselling
Creative Writing
Cricket
Croatian
Crystal Healing
CVs
Czech
Danish
Decluttering
Desktop Publishing
Detox
Digital Home Movie Making
Digital Photography
Dog Training
Drawing

Dream Interpretation
Dutch
Dutch Conversation
Dutch Dictionary
Dutch Grammar
Eastern Philosophy
Electronics
English as a Foreign Language
English Grammar
English Grammar as a Foreign Language
Entrepreneurship
Estonian
Ethics
Excel 2003
Feng Shui
Film Making
Film Studies
Finance for Non-Financial Managers
Finnish
First World War, The
Fitness
Flash 8
Flash MX
Flexible Working
Flirting
Flower Arranging
Franchising
French
French Conversation
French Dictionary
French for Homebuyers
French Grammar
French Phrasebook
French Starter Kit
French Verbs
French Vocabulary
Freud
Gaelic
Gaelic Conversation
Gaelic Dictionary
Gardening
Genetics
Geology
German
German Conversation

German Grammar
German Phrasebook
German Starter Kit
German Vocabulary
Globalization
Go
Golf
Good Study Skills
Great Sex
Green Parenting
Greek
Greek Conversation
Greek Phrasebook
Growing Your Business
Guitar
Gulf Arabic
Hand Reflexology
Hausa
Herbal Medicine
Hieroglyphics
Hindi
Hindi Conversation
Hinduism
History of Ireland, The
Home PC Maintenance and
   Networking
How to DJ
How to Run a Marathon
How to Win at Casino Games
How to Win at Horse Racing
How to Win at Online Gambling
How to Win at Poker
How to Write a Blockbuster
Human Anatomy & Physiology
Hungarian
Icelandic
Improve Your French
Improve Your German
Improve Your Italian
Improve Your Spanish
Improving Your Employability
Indian Head Massage
Indonesian
Instant French
Instant German
Instant Greek
Instant Italian

Instant Japanese
Instant Portuguese
Instant Russian
Instant Spanish
Internet, The
Irish
Irish Conversation
Irish Grammar
Islam
Israeli-Palestinian Conflict, The
Italian
Italian Conversation
Italian for Homebuyers
Italian Grammar
Italian Phrasebook
Italian Starter Kit
Italian Verbs
Italian Vocabulary
Japanese
Japanese Conversation
Java
JavaScript
Jazz
Jewellery Making
Judaism
Jung
Kama Sutra, The
Keeping Aquarium Fish
Keeping Pigs
Keeping Poultry
Keeping a Rabbit
Knitting
Korean
Latin
Latin American Spanish
Latin Dictionary
Latin Grammar
Letter Writing Skills
Life at 50: For Men
Life at 50: For Women
Life Coaching
Linguistics
LINUX
Lithuanian
Magic
Mahjong
Malay

Managing Stress
Managing Your Own Career
Mandarin Chinese
Mandarin Chinese Conversation
Marketing
Marx
Massage
Mathematics
Meditation
Middle East Since 1945, The
Modern China
Modern Hebrew
Modern Persian
Mosaics
Music Theory
Mussolini's Italy
Nazi Germany
Negotiating
Nepali
New Testament Greek
NLP
Norwegian
Norwegian Conversation
Old English
One-Day French
One-Day French – the DVD
One-Day German
One-Day Greek
One-Day Italian
One-Day Polish
One-Day Portuguese
One-Day Spanish
One-Day Spanish – the DVD
One-Day Turkish
Origami
Owning a Cat
Owning a Horse
Panjabi
PC Networking for Small
 Businesses
Personal Safety and Self
 Defence
Philosophy
Philosophy of Mind
Philosophy of Religion
Phone French
Phone German

Phone Italian
Phone Japanese
Phone Mandarin Chinese
Phone Spanish
Photography
Photoshop
PHP with MySQL
Physics
Piano
Pilates
Planning Your Wedding
Polish
Polish Conversation
Politics
Portuguese
Portuguese Conversation
Portuguese for Homebuyers
Portuguese Grammar
Portuguese Phrasebook
Postmodernism
Pottery
PowerPoint 2003
PR
Project Management
Psychology
Quick Fix French Grammar
Quick Fix German Grammar
Quick Fix Italian Grammar
Quick Fix Spanish Grammar
Quick Fix: Access 2002
Quick Fix: Excel 2000
Quick Fix: Excel 2002
Quick Fix: HTML
Quick Fix: Windows XP
Quick Fix: Word
Quilting
Recruitment
Reflexology
Reiki
Relaxation
Retaining Staff
Romanian
Running Your Own Business
Russian
Russian Conversation
Russian Grammar
Sage Line 50

Sanskrit
Screenwriting
Second World War, The
Serbian
Setting Up a Small Business
Shorthand Pitman 2000
Sikhism
Singing
Slovene
Small Business Accounting
Small Business Health Check
Songwriting
Spanish
Spanish Conversation
Spanish Dictionary
Spanish for Homebuyers
Spanish Grammar
Spanish Phrasebook
Spanish Starter Kit
Spanish Verbs
Spanish Vocabulary
Speaking On Special Occasions
Speed Reading
Stalin's Russia
Stand Up Comedy
Statistics
Stop Smoking
Sudoku
Swahili
Swahili Dictionary
Swedish
Swedish Conversation
Tagalog
Tai Chi
Tantric Sex
Tap Dancing
Teaching English as a Foreign
  Language
Teams & Team Working
Thai
Thai Conversation
Theatre
Time Management
Tracing Your Family History
Training
Travel Writing
Trigonometry

Turkish
Turkish Conversation
Twentieth Century USA
Typing
Ukrainian
Understanding Tax for Small
  Businesses
Understanding Terrorism
Urdu
Vietnamese
Visual Basic
Volcanoes, Earthquakes and
  Tsunamis
Watercolour Painting
Weight Control through Diet &
  Exercise
Welsh
Welsh Conversation
Welsh Dictionary
Welsh Grammar
Wills & Probate
Windows XP
Wine Tasting
Winning at Job Interviews
Word 2003
World Faiths
Writing Crime Fiction
Writing for Children
Writing for Magazines
Writing a Novel
Writing a Play
Writing Poetry
Xhosa
Yiddish
Yoga
Your Wedding
Zen
Zulu

teach yourself	**green parenting** lynoa cattanach

- Do you want advice on natural pregnancy and birth?
- Do you want to be an environmentally aware parent?
- Would you like a happy, healthy and balanced family?

Green Parenting is a practical guide to making informed, ethically aware choices for your family. It covers all elements of domestic life, from children and nappies to travel and toys, offering step-by-step advice and useful suggestions for every level of interest and commitment.

Lynoa Cattanach is a director of BabyGROE, a charity promoting a parent-friendly approach to a greener life through its magazines and website.